SOFT JEWELRY:
Design, Techniques, Materials

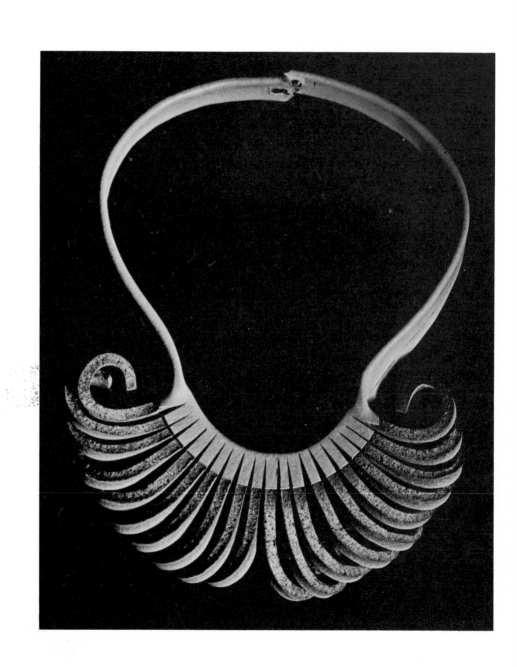

Nancy Howell-Koehler

SOFT JEWELRY:
Design, Techniques,
Materials

Davis Publications, Inc.
Worcester, Massachusetts

Copyright 1976
Davis Publications, Inc.
Worcester, Massachusetts, U.S.A.

Printed in the United States of America
Library of Congress Catalog Card
Number: 75-41546
ISBN 0-87192-081-6

Printing: Davis Press, Inc.
Binding: Halliday Lithographers
Type: Palatino
Graphic Design: Penny Darras,
Thumbnail Associates

Consulting Editors: George F. Horn and
Sarita R. Rainey

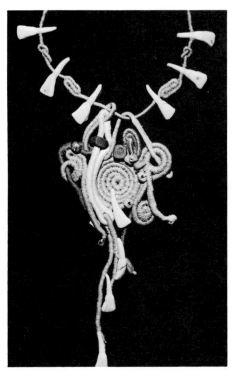

Basketry necklace with mules' teeth and
ceramic beads. Artist, B. J. Adams.

Illustrations:
Cover — Macramé, Helen Bitar.
Page 1 — Macramé necklace mounted on
choker wire. Artist, Amy Kayes.
Page 2 — Neckpiece by Rex Lingwood.

10   9   8   7   6   5   4   3   2   1

Contents

Appliquéd felt collar with mirror. Artist,
Julie Fatherley.

Foreword

The current surge of interest in all fiber techniques — weaving, knitting, macramé, crochet, braiding, basketry, and others — has been accompanied by a search by the artists for new uses of fabric and for contemporary forms for their designs. Knotted neck ornaments were some of the earliest and most innovative forms that the fiber artists created. Soon after the idea of knotted necklaces was conceived, designs for other forms of fiber jewelry, such as earrings, rings, bracelets, watch bands, etc. appeared. Also within a short time soft jewelry was made with other textile techniques besides macramé. Many of the designs that developed were colorful, some were delicate and lacy, others were large and dramatically sculptural. They either complimented or became the dominant interest of both men's and women's costume.

No doubt, some other culture has used fabric jewelry; however, it is doubtful that it ever reached the importance of today's costume enrichment. Considering the combination of influences that exist now, we may have experienced only the beginning of these new fashion accessories. Contemporary fiber artists are curious, inventive, talented and unrestricted by convention. Authors who write good references such as this book will spark their imaginations and furnish the necessary technical information for them to develop even richer designs and more innovative forms of soft jewelry. It will be exciting to watch what happens.

Virginia Isham Harvey

Woven collar with tassels. Artist, Nelle
N. Rootes.

Chapter 1

Introduction

What is soft jewelry? How can jewelry be soft? These are the questions most often asked by those who are fascinated by the apparent contradiction in terms of the phrase, "soft jewelry."

Soft jewelry is lively, adventurous and non-restrictive. It uses the human form as its sculptural model around which all other forms are created. Most importantly, it opens up avenues of expression, enabling the novice jewelry designer, as well as the skilled craftsman, to find satisfying solutions.

As art to be worn, soft jewelry is basic to our concept of what contemporary jewelry is or should be. Jewelry need not be limited to expensive metals or rare jewels — for its validity is based upon the communication of a design idea, not the materials from which it was created.

Materials for soft jewelry are not specialized in any real sense. They are defined as "soft" not by their textural qualities alone, but through their application. Materials that can be woven, wrapped, crocheted, knotted or stitched comprise the majority of the materials we categorize as "soft." These materials are often common to our everyday lives and include yarns and fabrics, feathers, leather, plastic in many forms, natural materials and others.

As the designer begins to explore the media, the term soft jewelry takes on a more personal meaning. Each individual's definition will differ as a concept becomes a finished work.

Leather wrist band adorned with brass wire. Student, grade 7.

Stitched and stuffed suede collar with appliquéd braid. Artist, the author.

Necklace created on inkle loom. Artist, Ruth Ann Coleman.

Knotted necklace with feathers, ostrich shell, clay and stone beads. Artist, Suzanne Kores.

Chapter 2

Choosing Materials for Soft Jewelry Design

Choosing materials for soft jewelry is an enjoyable task, particularly when the designer remains open-minded and flexible. Designs need not be dependent upon the use of exotic components, but can be built around the innovative use of every-day materials. Each material, whether it be ordinary knitting yarn or a plush suede, should be sought out, investigated and experienced in its own right.

Designs often grow spontaneously from the selection of and involvement with materials of all types. The selection process may begin by simply gathering available materials and discovering possible relationships. Or, it may require searching for specific materials to fulfill a preconceived design idea. Whatever the method used, materials often provide the inspiration for the final design.

Fabric

Today's textile industry produces fabrics of almost every color, texture and pattern imaginable. For this reason the search for the right fabric or combination of fabrics can be an intriguing but sometimes frustrating experience. Before making a selection of fabrics for jewelry design, begin working with a collection of sample fabrics, each one displaying a different texture, color or pattern. The initial collection need not be extensive nor expensive, but can grow from an accumulation of sewing scraps or discarded cloth-ing. Add to the initial collection by actively searching out interesting fabrics from many sources. As the collection grows and various types of fabrics are handled and compared, inherent relationships in color, pattern and texture will emerge. Jewelry design can then proceed in a spontaneous manner as an outgrowth of involvement with fabrics.

Bargain fabrics can be found in most fabric shops which feature "end of the bolt" offerings of limited yardage. Second-hand clothing stores are a good source of inexpensive fabrics which reflect, through their texture and patterns, the fashion era in which they were produced. Older scraps of fabrics, such as quilt patches and old lace, are often available in many antique shops. Fabrics with exotic textures can also be obtained from specialty upholstery shops whose proprietors are willing to sell scraps and sample swatch books. Trading fabric scraps

A collection of patterned fabrics contains many different designs and colors.

with friends who regularly sew is another possibility.

Fabric choices will become more manageable when they are made in respect to the potentials and limitations of the fabric itself. Knowledge of the structure, weight, texture, color and pattern enables the designer to confidently plan a jewelry design.

Structure and Weight

The structure of a fabric will depend upon its original construction. Fabrics are woven, knitted or fused. The weight of fabric relates to its structure and also to the fibers from which it was produced. Lightweight fabrics differ from heavy fabrics in the number of fibers per square inch as well as in the thickness of their ply. For example, a plain woven cloth of 2-ply cotton will be heavier than the identical weave using 2-ply silk.

A necklace made with feathers and other materials exemplifies the artist's ability to integrate different materials into a unified design statement. Artist, Catherine Crossman. Photograph by Walt Peterson.

Printed, lightweight cotton was stitched and stuffed to create small pillow-like triangular forms and then integrated into a necklace. Artist, Julie Fatherley.

The structure of a fabric will influence jewelry design and construction. For example, felt is a fused fabric of tightly matted fibers. It has good body and will not fray, but it is comparatively difficult to hand stitch. Bonding or machine stitching are superior methods for felt constructions. Hand stitching is feasible when applying decoration. Fabrics with loosely woven structures are more likely to fray and, therefore, are usually constructed with machine stitched seams. Synthetic bonded knit fabrics represent still another set of structural characteristics which must be dealt with if they are to be used for jewelry.

The weight of fabric chosen for soft jewelry will, in most cases, be reflected in the final design solution. For instance, a finely woven, lightweight fabric lacks the body needed to create sculptural forms. Lightweight cotton, silk, satin, organdy, chiffon and voile are suitable for jewelry when used in conjunction with heavier bodied fabrics or when strengthened with padding, stuffing, or layering. Heavier, closely woven fabrics allow for simpler construction methods. They can be expected to retain their original shape, strength and body and provide a background for less stable materials.

Texture

Texture is one of the primary motivational aspects of fabric. It is the texture that gives fabric its unique surface appeal, both to the eye and to the touch. Jewelry designed from fabrics should reflect these textural qualities.

Highly textured fabrics require different design solutions than less textured fabrics. Heavy brocade, corduroy, wool and synthetic fur make strong design statements in their own right. They have depth and form which should be emphasized, not overshadowed. Highly textured fabrics are rarely used as backgrounds on which other materials are to be placed; but work best when used in conjunction with less textured material to intensify contrasts. Fabrics with a shiny or plush surface accentuate form in three-dimensional jewelry elements. Smooth, evenly textured fabrics provide more of a neutral background on which to create patterns of appliqué or stitchery.

In addition to the more technical design considerations, texture is vital to the emotional impact of a piece. Glowing satins and shimmering lamés suggest elegance, while denim, burlap and muslin are more "earthy" in quality. Organdy, chiffon and voile have an airy quality.

Heavy tweeds and thick wools are more massive.

The visual, tactual and emotional appeal of textured fabrics, combined with the designer's personal involvement with the fabric, can result in an exciting exploration of textures in ordinary material. The orderly texture of white linen inspired the stitchery in the work by artist Bucky King. The interior sections of the fabric were manipulated, stitched, cut and bound. Beads and couching were added to build textural variety. Finally, the design was rimmed in fringe, created by separating the woven fibers to expose the natural texture of the linen.

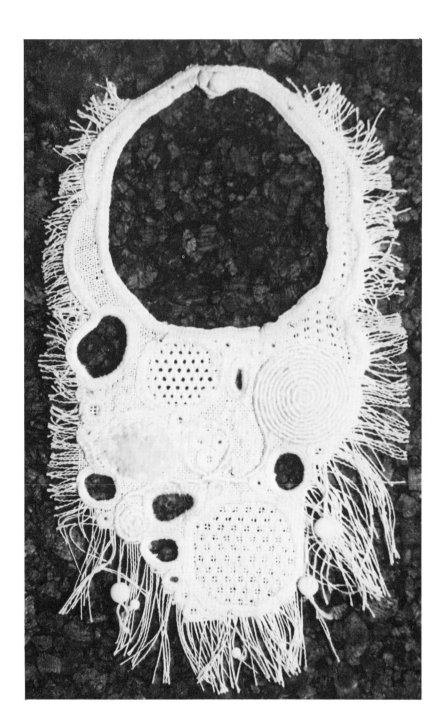

Stitchery, beads and couching were combined in the creation of this white linen collar. Artist, Bucky King.

Three-color silkscreen printed fabric is
the basis of freeform stuffed and quilted
neckpiece. Artist, the author.

Hand Printed Fabrics

The simplest, easiest printing techniques are applicable to fabrics. Printing can be accomplished on any reasonably flat surface that will accept ink. Consequently there are a number of handy household articles that are appropriate for experimentation. Raw vegetables, synthetic sponges and potato mashers are only a few items which have been successfully used. Several different items may be tested for printing clarity before a final shape or combination of shapes are chosen for the printed pattern.

A more detailed, overall pattern can be achieved with linoleum or wood block printing. Both of these methods require that the negative space in the design be cut away, allowing the areas that remain to be inked and printed.

All hard surface printing techniques tend to produce more or less fuzzy lines. When hard-edged, multicolored designs are desired, silkscreen printing must be used. There are several procedures involved in the preparation of a screen for printing, but basically this type of reproduction relies on simple stencil resist principles. Ink passes through the open or unmasked areas of the screen onto the fabric. Silkscreen is the most reliable and professional method for printing an overall fabric pattern, though it does require a great deal of planning to insure perfect registration for interlocking patterns in the design.

Hand-dyed Fabrics

Hand-dyed fabric greatly extends the number of patterns available for soft jewelry design. Tie-dying produces subtle figured fabrics, while batik offers a more controlled pattern and color.

Tie-dying is a simple resist method in which the areas to be protected from the dye bath are folded or twisted and then wrapped with cord and tied. After the fabric has been dipped or submerged into the dye bath, it is removed, rinsed and dried. The cords are then cut and the pattern examined. When a multicolored pattern is desired, the process of tying and dying is repeated a number of times.

Tie-dying is most effective when used with sheer fabric. The airy quality of the fabric is enhanced by the spreading colors of the tie-dyed patterns. One approach to jewelry created for tie-dyed fabrics can be seen in the illustrated necklace which employs both tie-dyed and batik dyed patterns. The feathery pattern of the tie-dying contrasts with the bolder pattern of batik, while the strings or ties deliberately left on the fabric produce textural variety.

Circular tie-dyed and stitched shapes are adaptable as pendant shapes for jewelry. Artist, Doris Flores.

Necklace of tie-dyed and batiked fabric. Ties are left in place as ornamentation. Student artist, Oregon College of Education. Instructor, Ruth Culbertson.

Batik dying is also a resist method which depends upon wax to block out those areas which are not to receive dye. Hot wax is painted or drawn upon the fabric before it is submerged in the dye. Several applications of wax between succeeding dye baths of increasingly deeper intensity should be used to build up patterns of great complexity and depth.

Batik fabrics need not be translucent, but their selection should be based on the capacity to accept dyes. Before dying begins, a sample swatch should be prepared to test dye color and determine wax absorption.

Patterns used for batik might be preplanned around a jewelry design. More spontaneously created patterns may become an inspiration for soft jewelry. Whatever the direction, the success of the batik pattern will depend upon its total integration into the design statement. For example, the illustrated quilted necklace is composed of organic shapes which compliment the pattern in the dyed fabric. The batik pattern is further defined by the use of quilting. The harmony of the gently curving lines and patterns adds unity to the total design.

Quilted batik neckpiece. Student artist, Oregon College of Education. Instructor, Ruth Culbertson.

An assortment of threads, yarns and cords.

Fiber

Included within the category of fibers, both natural and synthetic, is an enormous variety of materials ranging from fibers in their raw state to spun yarn, thread, cord and rope.

Fibers for soft jewelry may be obtained from many different sources. Relatively inexpensive fibers, namely knitting yarn, crochet and sewing thread, packaging twine and cord are available at department and variety stores. The choice of texture may be limited, but color selection is usually good.

More specialized knitting yarns, weaving yarns and macramé cord are available from specialty yarn shops or craft shops with large fiber selections.

Novelty yarns, metallic fibers, raw fiber and heavy gauge cord can be difficult to find locally and often must be ordered from suppliers who specialize in fibers for craftsmen and handweavers. Send for their catalog and when possible purchase a sample card to experience color and textures of the yarn firsthand. Several mail order suppliers can be found in the back of the book.

The dramatic colors and inviting textures of yarns which make them so appealing also contribute to their expense. Building an extensive yarn collection takes time. Begin by choosing the most basic yarns. Add the textured and novelty yarns as the need for them arises. Buy yarns and fibers for a pre-determined purpose. Select yarn color, texture and ply in accordance with the techniques to be used. For instance, stitchery will dictate many different yarn colors and textures, while crocheted designs might necessitate only one or two types of fiber. Yarns for weaving are varied and will depend upon the thickness of warp and loom design. Macramé usually requires one or more colors of identical textured cord.

Restrictions imposed by a limited yarn selection can usually be overcome. When a yarn of several different thicknesses or plies is needed, multi-ply yarn can be separated. Conversely, several strands of thin yarn can be twisted together when heavier yarn is desired. Either method insures color uniformity.

Depending upon the design, it will not always be possible to collect all the necessary fibers before the work takes shape. As the design progresses and new relationships are discovered, additional yarns can be purchased to meet precise requirements.

Textured woolen and acrylic yarns were allowed to fringe around woven collar to create a dramatic textural piece adorned with turkey feathers and a carved walnut toggle. Artist, Nelle N. Rootes.

Structure and Weight

The individual structures of both natural and synthetic fibers are unique. This continues to be true after single strands have been spun together into lengths of thread or yarn. The longer the single fiber, the stronger the yarn, but the actual strength of the yarn is rarely an important factor in choosing yarn for jewelry, except in special cases (i.e. warp thread for weaving.)

However, the weight of spun yarns and threads is relevant to jewelry design and construction. The weight or thickness of an individual piece of yarn will depend upon its original composition of spun fibers, plus the number of strands or plies twisted together to create the yarn. For example, a four-ply wool yarn is thicker than a two-ply wool yarn, making the four-ply more suitable for use in stitchery on loosely woven fabric, for fringe and rya techniques. Thinner two-ply wool yarns are versatile and can be used for stitchery, weaving, needlepoint and appliqué. Novelty yarns with uneven strength and thickness exhibit a more limited use, but are desirable when creating textured weaves for jewelry.

Neckpiece of raw sisal wrapped with rayon and cotton cord. Artist, Merle H. Sykora. Photograph by Gerald Korte.

Texture

Texture is possibly the most important characteristic of fibers from the designer's point of view. Designing with fiber is really building with texture. This is also true in soft jewelry. The texture of the fibers, along with the color of the yarn, establishes the mood and determines design relationships in the final work. Depth and dimension are created through the use of visual contrasts in texture. Coarse, textured fibers appear closer when used in conjunction with smooth fibers that seemingly fade into the background. Eye-catching contrasts of texture and color produce areas of interest around which patterns develop. The focal point of other designs might rely on the obvious tactual quality of a fiber. An example of a design based on textural emphasis is seen in the wrapped neckpiece by Merle Sykora. Here the coarse quality of the sisal is heightened by the smoothly wrapped portions of cotton and rayon yarn. Although the proportion of highly textured material is a small part of the total design, the texture of sisal is the visually dominant force of the neckpiece.

Using variety in texture to make a strong statement in contrast is only one approach. An alternative might be to focus attention on a single texture throughout a work. To accomplish this the most identifiable characteristic should be singled out and then amplified by the design process. For example, smooth textured rayon cord continues to reflect light even after it is tied into a macramé neckpiece. Lamé cord will retain its metallic quality when it has been crocheted into jewelry. The three-dimensional shapes in the necklace suggest subtle textural differences; yet, the texture of the fiber retains its identity in the final work.

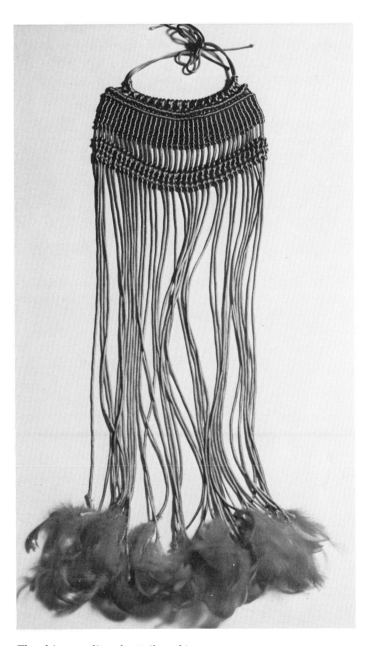

The shiny quality of rattail cord is enhanced by the knotted pattern in this macramé necklace with feathers. Artist, Dolly Curtis. Photograph by Jack Curtis.

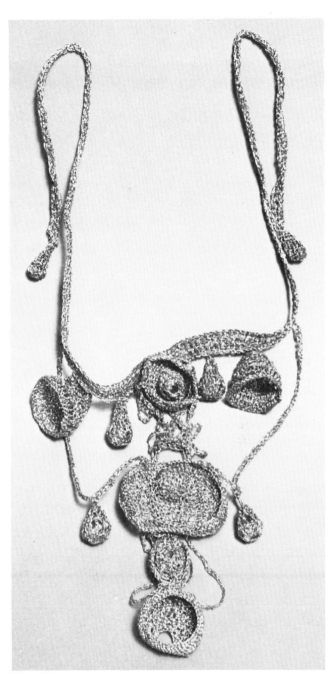

Crocheted lamé necklace. Artist, Mary Lou Higgins. Photograph by Edward Koelling Higgins.

Color

Color and color combinations are exciting aspects of working with fibers. The texture of fiber brings to each color a special depth, causing colors of the same hue and intensity to appear differently on each type of fiber. This becomes obvious when comparing a piece of blue jute yarn with the identical color of nylon yarn.

In addition to the actual hue, tone and intensity of color, colors affect individuals differently. Color selection is not solely objective, but relates to the way in which an individual perceives color. Color preferences that might limit the use of color should become a point of departure for experimentation with more unusual color combinations.

When making a color selection, the dominant color or color combinations are usually chosen first. Other colors are added to intensify areas, create depth or heighten contrasts as the design progresses.

Generally speaking, graduations of one color are used when a restful harmonious quality is desired, while vibrant colors with high contrast intensity are usually more visually exciting. Balanced color repetition can become monotonous, while random repetition provides a unifying effect as the eye sees and connects color patterns.

An example of random use of color patterns is seen in the illustration of the woven collar. The dark, light and medium intensities and their relationships can be examined in the black and white photo. The integration of intensities leads the eye back and forth through the design as it reinforces the linear quality of the collar and gives unity to the entire piece.

Tapestry woven collar. Artist, Bucky King.

Assortment of different grades and colors of leather.

Leather

Leather is used for hundreds of products, ranging from shoes to furniture to overcoats. The great versatility of this material makes it a particularly challenging choice for soft jewelry. Because of the many grades, weights and textures, ranging from the supple and easy-to-handle suedes to coarse and unyielding rawhides, the uses of leather in jewelry design are diverse.

Leather can be purchased in craft shops and even shoe repair shops, but for the inexperienced leather worker a visit to a specialty leather shop may be more productive. Here the comparison of different grades of leather suitable for jewelry making will aid in the selection.

In addition to large pieces of leather, most shops also sell scraps for a fraction of the cost of uncut pieces. Exploring a leather scrap bin can provide an exciting tactile experience while uncovering interesting positive and negative patterns that can be incorporated into jewelry. Punched ovals, V's, circles and C's, or the surrounding leather from which these shapes were taken, can become design units in themselves, suggesting ideas for jewelry.

Grades, Weights and Textures

Different grades of leather are taken from different animals and processed into various weights and textures. The individual structure of each grade of leather suggests its usage for jewelry. For example, the texture of suede exhibits a supple, moving quality. Because suede is easily cut and stitched, it is an excellent choice for sewn or appliqued creations. It can be patched together either by lacing or stitching. It might also be stuffed and quilted in the manner of heavy fabric. Whatever the design solution, the unique texture of suede should remain a dominant aspect in the design.

An example of a design built around the textural qualities of suede is seen in *Collar with Cows' Teeth*. Contrasts in the texture of the yarn and the cows' teeth amplify the visual appeal of the leather. Repetition of the smaller design elements arranged around the organic leather form provides unity of shape and materials.

Collar With Cow's Teeth. Student artist,
St. Cloud State College. Instructor,
Merle H. Sykora. Photograph by Gerald
Korte.

Necklace designed from many small cut leather shapes. Artist, Ingeborg Pfriemer, Munich, Germany.

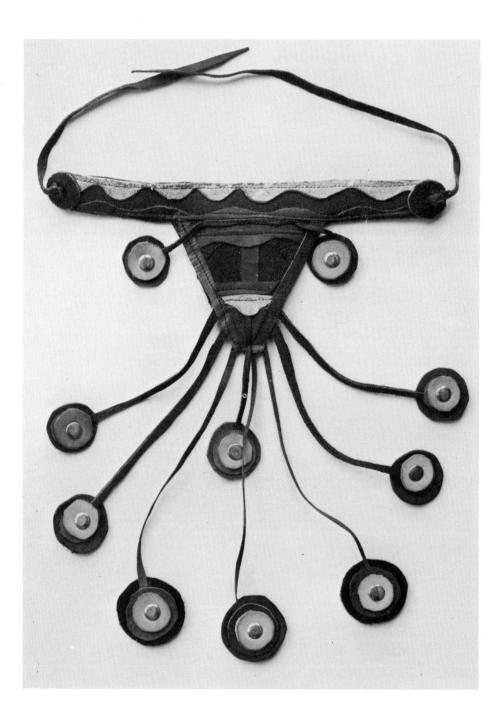

Heavier grades of leather such as cowhide imply strength, solidarity and sculptural form. These grades will require more traditional techniques associated with leather working. Heavy leather can be cut with a matte knife. However, stitching is not always practical and the shapes can be joined by gluing, lacing or with metal brads.

The weight, pliability and textural surface of leather are important qualities in jewelry design. These components have been successfully combined in the leather neckpiece by Rex Lingwood. Created from one piece of leather, cut and wet molded by hand, the neckpiece contrasts the smoothness of the tanned surface with the roughness of the reverse side. This contrast is made even more obvious by the subtle molding of the cut linear shapes which make up the body of the piece.

Pattern

Leather is a natural material with natural patterns of grain. However, these natural patterns of grain are not equally visible in all types of leather. Deeply grained leathers are used to obtain overall textural quality. Smooth textured leathers lend themselves to the application of decorative patterning.

The pliable surface of leather is ideal for various types of patterning. Tooling, burning, stamping, carving, embossing and stippling are all patterning techniques which may be used separately or combined according to the jewelry design.

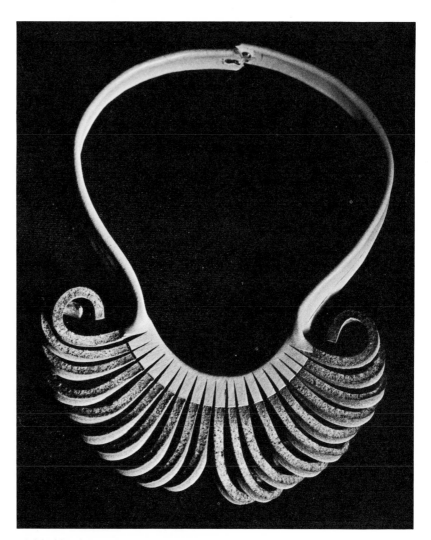

Molded leather neckpiece with curled fringe. Artist, Rex Lingwood, Halifax, Nova Scotia, Canada.

The center of this leather pendant was tooled with a carpenter's finishing nail. Metal buttons fasten suede and decorate pendant. Student artist, grade 11.

Multimedia necklace of stuffed forms
and macramé. Artist, Jean S. Battles.

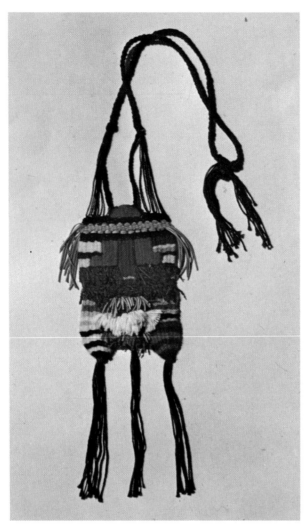

Charles' Volvo Tapestry Necklace. Loom woven. Millie Hines.

Patchwork pendant. Artist, Rose Dwight.

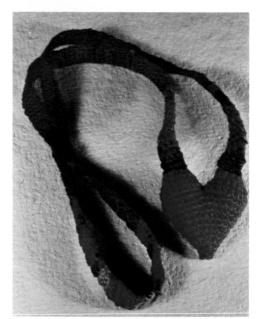

Crocheted heart-shaped necklace. Artist, Renie Breskin Adams.

Appliquéd collar of felt. Artist, Julie
Fatherley.

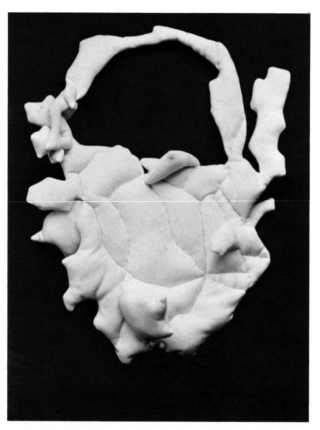

Freeform stuffed and stitched necklace.
Artist, Yoshiko Daniel.

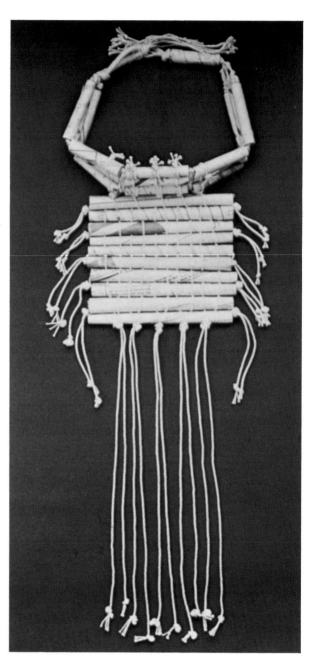

Knotted cord over rolled newspaper.
Artist, Marjorie Schick.

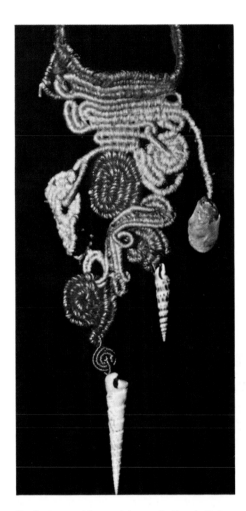

Basketry necklace with sea shells, Artist,
B. J. Adams.

Fetish neckpiece of leather, twigs, bam-
boo, feather and fur. Artist, John Ceder-
quist.

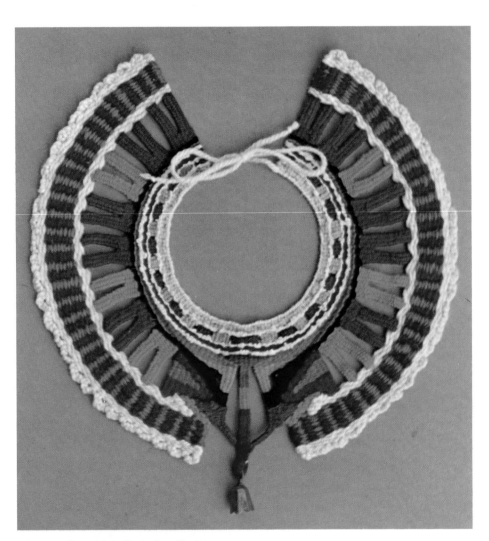

Woven collar with bell. Artist, Christena
Weber.

To Make A Point . . . . Knotted tapestry pendant. Artist, the author.

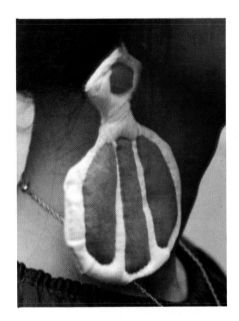

Earrings from stuffed and stitched silk screen fabric. Artist, Joan Tallen.

Acrylic Fibula. Mixed media neckpiece with stuffed gingham ties. Artist, Gerry Evans.

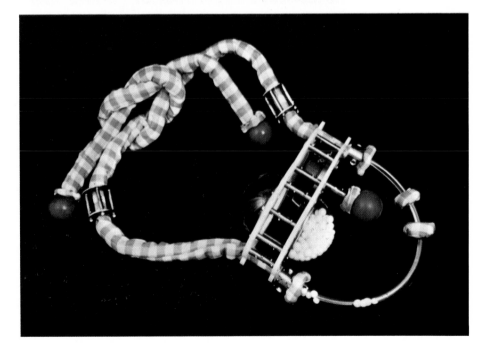

Multicolored macramé neckpiece. Artist, Helen Bitar.

Leather neckpiece shaped by hand forming. Artist, Rex Lingwood. Halifax, Nova Scotia, Canada.

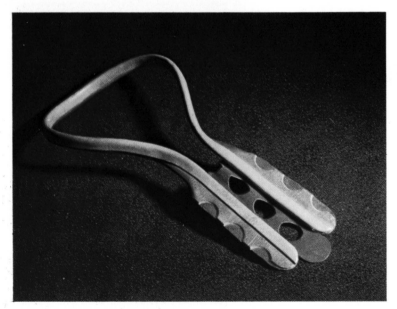

There are many specialized tools designed to create patterns in leather. These tools are available at specialty leather shops, but are not absolutely necessary. Simple substitutes such as spoons, knives, keys, screw drivers and other metal objects lend themselves to tooling. The surface of the leather can be carved with a matte knife or linoleum cutting tools. Pointed and rounded ceramic tools are useful for stippling and embossing. Detailed patterning is also possible with an inexpensive wood burning pencil. Anything which carves into, indents or embosses the surface of leather can be adapted for use as a patterning tool.

To produce a suitable leather pattern, experiment with different tools on leather scraps. After a pleasing pattern is achieved, transfer the outline onto tracing paper. The paper should then be placed over water-moistened leather and traced with a pencil or tracing tool.

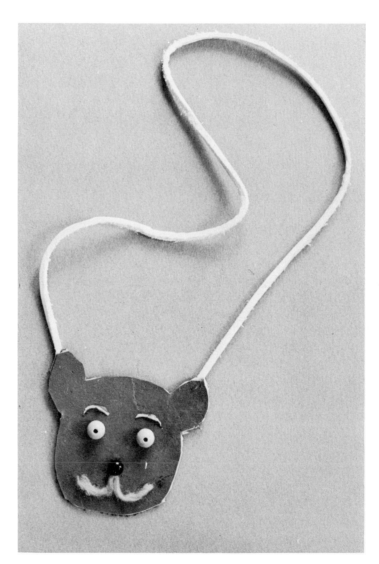

Animal face cut from heavy grade leather and decorated with leather scraps, beads and yarn. Student, grade 7.

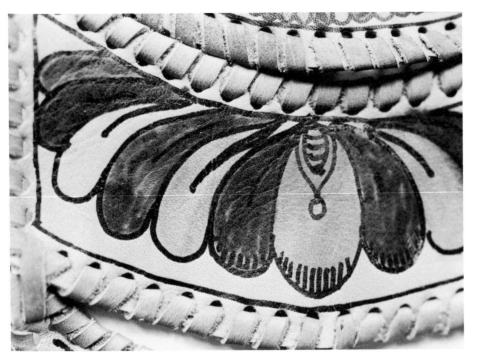

Detail of design using red, green,
orange and black leather dyes.

Color

The porosity of leather permits it to
accept dyes readily. With the exception of suedes, which are best purchased in the color desired, most
leathers absorb dyes evenly.

When an all-over color is needed,
special leather dyes are recommended. Dyes should be applied
with smooth even strokes using an
applicator or a piece of cheesecloth.

Designs using pieces of colored
leather can be equated with designs
using colored fabric swatches. That
is, colored leather may be assem-
bled into multicolored collages or
patchwork designs, depending
upon the designer's individual de-
termination of color and textural relationships.

As an alternative to assembling
colored leather pieces, colorful designs can be applied directly to the
surface of the leather. Several types
of paint, ink and dye are marketed
for this purpose and the choice will
depend upon the intricacy of the
patterns and the depth of color desired. Leather dyes can be painted
on an area within a design by using
a fine brush. Most leather dyes are
semi-transparent after the initial
coating and can be reapplied to obtain a more opaque color. However,
when an opaque color is preferable,
an acrylic paint will be the best
medium. Marking pens of various
colors are also very practical for
drawing intricate designs on leather
and can be applied in conjunction
with tooled or embossed patterns.

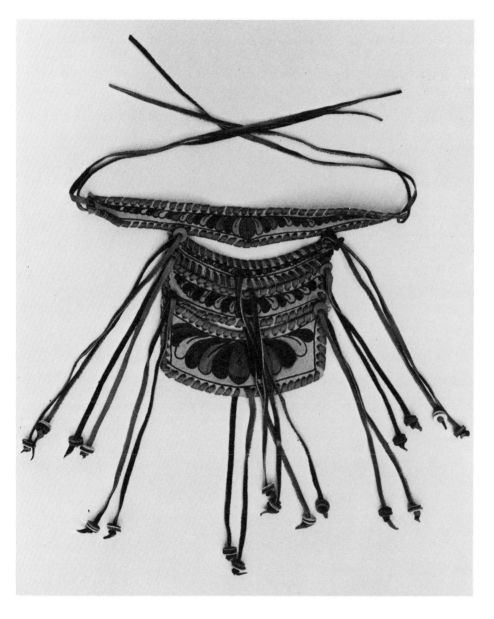

Leather necklace with painted design.
Artist, contemporary Mexican craftsperson, Oaxaca, Mexico.

Found Materials

Found materials offer the designer a world of interesting shapes, textures and forms from which to create or decorate soft jewelry. It is this enormous range of materials and products, both natural and synthetic, that challenges the imaginative designer. Free materials that can be found and adapted to fulfill specific functions represent one of the most rewarding experiences in the design process.

As the designer begins to search out materials, general needs can be identified. First, will this material become a basic building block of the design, or will the material contribute primarily to its visual impact? Second, will a variety of similar materials be selected from which one primary material is chosen, or is the requirement so specific that a single material must be used? Keep in mind that these are merely suggestions. There is no one right way to select materials. It is possible to reverse the entire process. The found materials may in themselves become design inspirations.

Although found materials are separated in this text into two headings which deal with their function within a design, this does not mean that their use is restricted. Many materials are overlapping in their functions. They are decorative as well as useful in construction and could possibly fulfill both needs in one composition.

Assortment of found materials that might be used for jewelry.

Necklace of polystyrene packing material strung on fine wire. Artist, Susan L. Williams.

Fabric petals for *Sunflower Necklace* were formed around shapes cut from a discarded polystyrene packaging tray. Artist, B. J. Adams.

Detail of polystyrene shapes.

Materials for Jewelry Construction

A multitude of materials can become the underlying structure of a jewelry design. Of these, cardboard and plastic products are easily obtained and most frequently used.

These materials are easily cut into shapes that will provide an underlying armature around which the three-dimensional forms are constructed. And although these materials are rarely visible, they can impart shape and stability to fiber and fabric components. Cut shapes may be inserted into woven or crocheted work as the design progresses, or can be padded and covered with fabric or suede.

Individual shapes are first drawn directly on the foundation material, then cut and refined to meet design specifications. The illustrated *Sunflower Necklace* is dependent on an inner structure of individual petals. Shapes cut from a polystyrene meat tray form the basic petal pattern. Using this shape as an outline, the fabric was cut somewhat larger to allow for padding. Also note that the seams are not visible in the finished work because the fabric overlaps the petal pattern. After the shapes are stuffed with padding, the fabric is stretched and hand-stitched to the lining on the back of each petal.

Amulet necklace of vinyl. Artist, Ramona Solberg.

When the desired shape cannot be made with cardboard and padding, Styrofoam balls and molded packaging material offer unlimited free form shapes for covering. Extruded polystyrene shapes present another alternative. Curved tubular and pellet shaped polystyrene is lightweight and may be covered, strung or integrated with other materials in a design.

Vinyls and similar plastic products are also practical for jewelry construction. Heavy grades of clear and opaque vinyls, found in plastic bags and scraps of upholstery covering, can be substituted for fabric in stitched and stuffed creations. The shiny surface of the vinyl evokes a totally different response than does a textured fabric and encourages new design solutions. Unlike fabrics, plastic vinyl is not limited to stitched or bonded construction, but may be heat-sealed to retain a smooth contemporary feeling. This type of construction is inflatable, making padding unnecessary.

Another advantage of vinyl, specifically crystal clear vinyl, is that intriguing materials may be encased inside heat-sealed shapes. The amulet necklace created by Ramona Solberg is an example of this approach. A combination of stitching and sealing was used to create compartments in which the individual materials are show-cased. The amulet is hung from a length of clear plastic tubing — another plastic product used in jewelry construction.

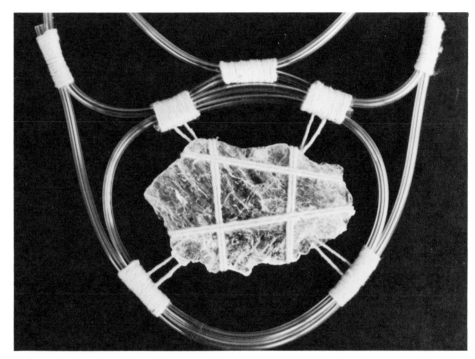

Detail showing clear plastic tubing in necklace by Roxanne Kukuk.

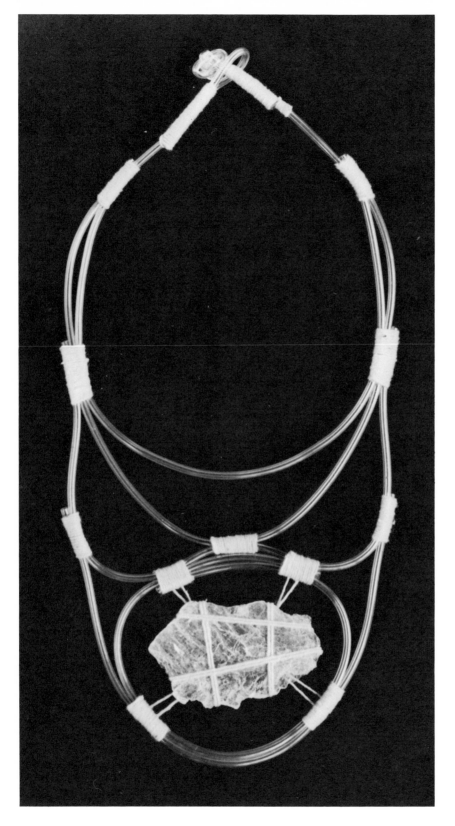

Mica necklace of wrapped clear plastic tubing. Artist, Roxanne Kukuk.

Novelty polyethylene packaging plastic provides the jewelry designer with unusual textures. Bubble plastic is one example of a material that can be adapted to several different applications. Shapes may be cut from sheets of plastic, then individual bubbles filled with decorative materials to form a tapestry of colors and textures. Bubble plastic distorts patterns which are laid underneath. To take advantage of this lens effect, bubble plastic can be attached to an underlying fabric whose pattern and color are enhanced by the distortion.

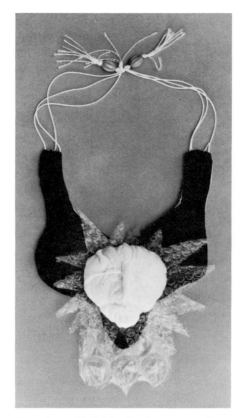

Two sizes of bubble plastic were used in sculptural neckpiece. Artist, Julie Fatherley.

Decorative Materials

Decorative materials can be defined as materials which are not absolutely essential to the construction of the jewelry, but which contribute to the decorative quality. This in no way implies that decorative materials are an afterthought, merely adding embellishment to an otherwise incomplete design. Instead, the selection and incorporation of decorative materials is an integral part of the ongoing design process.

The category of found decorative materials encompasses more than any one person could investigate. Natural materials, taken alone, are so varied and abundant that they could sustain a lifetime of exploration. The few examples considered here only hint at the broad realm for further exploration.

Natural Materials

Natural materials are widely accessible. Even city dwellers can collect rocks, find egg shells, or extract bones from cooked poultry and meats. It is during this act of searching for and collection of natural materials that the designer has an opportunity to experience the impact of the materials. The beauty of an object, its curious shape or its unusual color can spark the desire to preserve and incorporate even the simplest of materials. Seeds, nuts, leaves, fruit stones, tree bark, fossils and other commonplace things await the ingenious designer.

Woven collar with feathers. Artist, Nelle N. Rootes.

Both plain and patterned feathers fit beautifully into soft jewelry designs. Although it is sometimes possible to find feathers dropped by birds in flight, this source is limited. Visit aviaries, poultry farms and duck ponds to find feathers during the molting season. Second-hand stores sell feathers from old hats and craft shops often stock dyed poultry feathers.

The use of feathers in a design will be influenced by the size, shape, color and pattern of the feathers available. Usually, a limited number of feathers affords the most dramatic jewelry design. The example shown contains only five feathers. Each feather was carefully inserted into a cut piece of wooden dowel. The dowels were then wrapped with metal foil and bound to the body of the woven collar with matching yarn. The bright yellow feathers complement the yarns in the collar, while adding a textural dimension that could not be expressed with fiber alone.

Detail

Collar of Thai silk, pheasant feathers and glass beads. Student artist, St. Cloud State College. Instructor, Merle H. Sykora. Photograph by Gerald Korte.

A very different use of feathers can be seen in the Thai silk collar. A mass of feathers was used in close relationship to create a dramatic focal point, while secondary clusters of wrapped feathers move the eye around the circular portion of the stuffed collar.

Bone is another natural material, available in abundance. Its hard surface and naturally formed shapes make it an extremely interesting jewelry material. Of all the varieties available, small poultry bones are perhaps the easiest with which to work. They require little or no cutting. After they are properly cleaned and bleached (optional), they are ready for use.

A combination of small segmented bones can be seen in the wrapped necklace. The wrapped portion of the necklace appears to spring from the base of the design providing contrast to the wooden beads strung on exposed jute cord.

Larger beef and pork bones are also usable, but take more time to prepare. In addition to careful cleaning, large bones may require cutting, filing and polishing. A power band saw is best for slicing large bones into thin sections, while less precision cutting may be done with a hacksaw.

Egg shells, another discarded material, present a unique textural contribution to jewelry designs. The well-known technique of broken egg shell mosaics can be applied to padded fabric designs. Pieces of shell are first secured in place with a

Wrapped necklace with wooden beads and bones. Artist, B. J. Adams.

spot of glue and then surrounded by stitchery for an unusual approach to appliqué.

Sea shells are a much more durable material and provide a large assortment of textures, shapes and sizes. Holes can be drilled into small shells in order to mount them individually or string them into units. Other mounting options are gluing, or encasing them in fabric, leather or stitches. Large shells, otherwise too heavy and cumbersome for jewelry, can be sawed into sections or sliced in a manner similar to bone.

A combination of small shells and sliced sections of large shell were used in the illustrated macramé necklace. The entire pattern of cut shell sections echoes the chamber-like quality of the necklace. The smaller shells serve a functional role of holding the fastening cord in place, as well as contributing to the symmetry of the piéce.

Synthetic Materials

With the great surplus of "things" in the world today, jewelry adorned with someting that would otherwise be discarded is not only economically sound but also encourages the designer to look at his or her world in a different way. Designers who see lines, shapes, textures and forms present in found materials, regardless of their original function, will discover a wealth of material virtually at their fingertips.

Many pieces of scrap metal are suitable for jewelry embellishment. Found metal shapes such as punched

Macramé necklace with sea shells. Artist, Judy Hollinger.

pieces, springs, wire, containers, bands, balls, metal shavings are available from metal scrap yards and are generally sold by the pound. Other scraps of metal and plastic are available free to the collector. Wire, kitchen utensils, screws, nails, cans, mechanisms, or discarded clocks, radios, toys and appliances are only a few of the everyday household paraphernalia that can be employed in jewelry making.

The woven necklace created on a cardboard loom illustrates how punched-out metal shapes can influence the direction of an entire design. The circular woven elements radiate from the spoke-like configurations of the metal shapes. The textures and colors of the yarn create an illusion of space in which the metal pieces appear to float free.

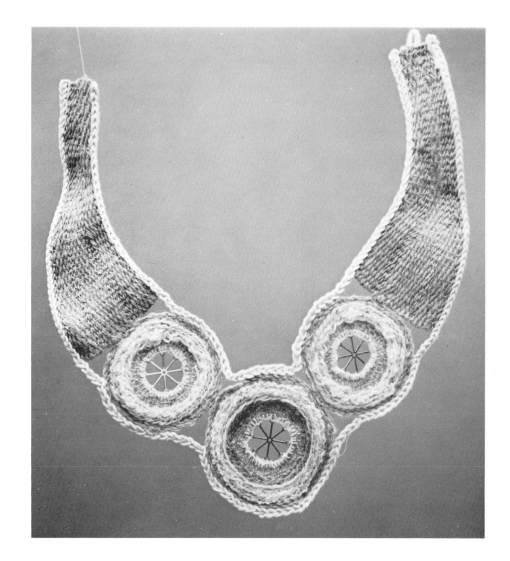

Soft woven necklace with metal inclusions. Student artist, Oregon College of Education. Instructor, Ruth Culbertson.

Metal Thread Work Collar. Artist, Bucky King.

The sewing basket is a great source of scrap materials around the home. It might contain buttons, buckles, broken strings of beads, old sequins, metallic braid, rick-rack, fringe, antique lace, small spools, metal eyelets and snaps that have been secreted away, waiting for just the right use. Perhaps no single item will inspire a work, but when combined into a collage of textures and shapes, they have the potential of becoming a very inventive piece. One such successful combination can be seen in *Metal Thread Work Collar*.

Found glass objects, tiny mirrors, bottle stoppers, small light bulbs, old radio tubes, cut glass from chandeliers, antique glass beads are all interesting glass objects that can be incorporated into jewelry with a minimum of adaptation. Tiny mirrors are easily stitched onto the surfaces or can also be encased in a framework of leather or fabric and bonded to the background. A collection of many types and sizes of old glass beads is often the starting point from which a design pro-

gresses. Used in a resourceful combination, perhaps with knotted patterns, beads lose their identity and reflect the unity present in the total design.

When all other sources fail, search the kitchen cupboard. Pasta of all kinds affords the designer a rare selection of shapes and textures that can be strung, stitched or glued. Pasta may also be painted with acrylics, poster paint or sprayed with enamels. Texture variations can be accentuated by wiping wet paint across the surface and allowing other areas to remain opaque.

Macrame necklace with a variety of glass beads. Artist, Virginia I. Harvey.

Chapter 3

Sources of Inspiration for Soft Jewelry Design

The design process in soft jewelry defies simple definition. Each designer brings to an individual work his or her unique background, technical skills and experience. The need to communicate a particular idea may be uppermost in the mind of one designer, while for another, the media becomes the message.

For some people, designs begin as an intuitive process. Materials are organized around an idea which grows and changes as inter-relationships become apparent. For others, the design process emanates from a predetermined idea. The final product is a replica of what appeared in the mind's eye of the designer. Still others combine both methods, improvising on a basic idea to arrive at a composite built around experimentation with a central theme.

The manner in which a designer may approach a design problem is diverse; the elements employed to create the design remain constant. There are the fixed visual elements used in planning and evaluating a design. They consist of line, texture, space, form, color, rhythm and balance and are applicable to every design problem in varying degrees.

Design Elements

Line

The designer, equipped with the ability to control line, can express moods as well as establish concrete ideas. Lines join and tie things together. They can provide direction, create tension, simulate movement and rhythm. Line variations may become the dominant force in a soft jewelry design.

The illustrated necklace of needle-woven and wrapped yarn is a study in line contrasts: thick and thin, diagonal and straight, curved and wavy, textured and smooth, colorful and plain. In the detailed photograph of one rectangular shape the interplay of lines becomes more obvious. Diagonal lines lead the eye across the center of the interior, while curved lines encompass the exterior and define shape. The vertical lines connecting the shapes are slightly curved allowing for a flow of continuity between the pieces.

The soft armlet created from layers of
dyed fabric is an innovative alternative
to more conventional bracelet designs.
Artist, Susan L. Williams.

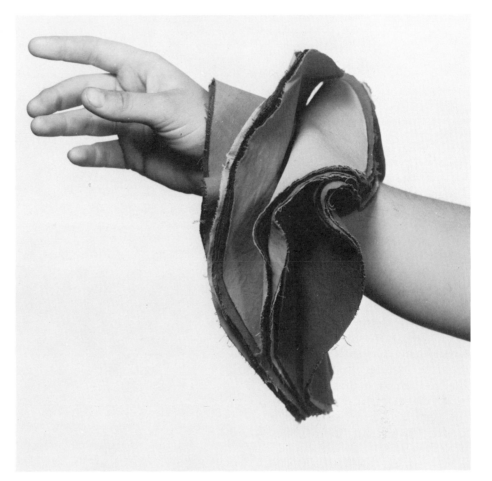

An interplay of lines dominate this
needle-woven and wrapped necklace of
fiber and beads. Artist, B. J. Adams.

Detail

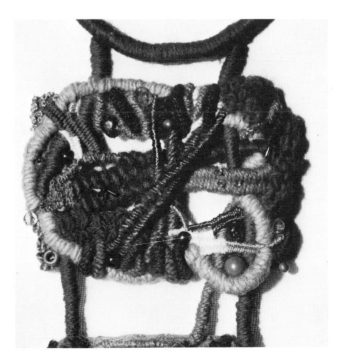

Texture

Texture is a vital element in the design of soft jewelry. Through the use of texture the designer is able to create illusions of space, emphasize visual patterns and produce areas of intense interest and variety.

Because rough surfaces reflect less light than smooth surfaces, the strategic use of color can heighten textural variety. A light reflective color in a densely textured material will have a far greater visual impact than the same material in a darker color.

In an example of this phenomenon, a woven collar combines several materials that are all textural in nature. The textural difference between the hand-spun wool and the synthetic bouclé yarn is made more apparent by the choice of colors and design placement. Patterns of lines and shapes also contribute to the textural variation.

Space

In design, the space existing around a shape is equally as important as the shape itself. This negative space that defines, separates and gives proportion to shapes and forms often exists unobserved. Although the interplay between the positive and negative design areas is essential in the creation of patterns of rhythm and balance, negative space is most obvious when it is not used

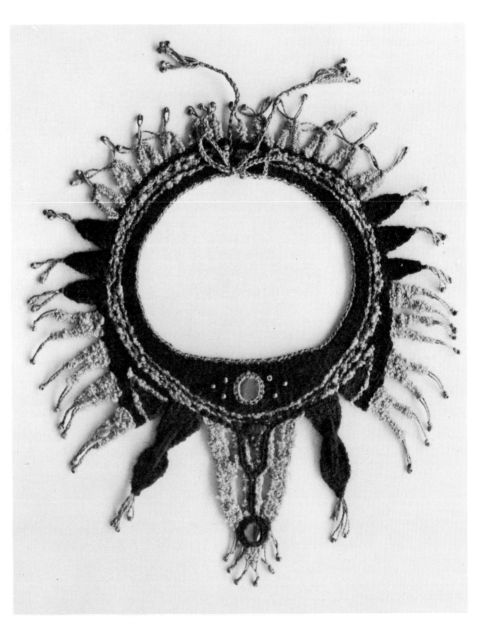

Color in this woven collar aids in heightening textural contrasts. Artist, Christena Weber.

54

correctly. Otherwise, balanced spatial relationships are a unifying factor in design.

The linen collar of needlepoint lace has an elegance borne of carefully planned patterns of positive and negative space. The neck opening and the space around the three dominant shapes all share a visual relationship to the elongated square in the body of the collar. The entire piece relies on an ordering of spatial proportions to establish its mood.

Balanced areas of positive and negative space are used in this needlepoint lace necklace design. Artist, Bucky King.

Strategic placement of contrasting colors
achieve depth and movement in the
embroidered pendant design. Artist,
Lynn Bassler.

Color

The element of color is critical to the success of soft jewelry designs. Because the areas of composition are relatively small, each color becomes increasingly important in its confined relationship to other colors in the design. In spite of this, some other aspects of working with color remain constant. Color complements, blends and harmonizes. Bright, intense colors attract attention and appear larger in area than do darker less obvious hues. Warm vibrant colors are emotionally exciting. Cool hues are more placid and restful.

Color is a highly personal choice for the designer who is prejudiced by an innate color sense and by social color conditioning. All of these factors, working in unison, produce highly individualized color combinations and although an understanding of the general principles governing color selection is important, it should be noted that almost any conceivable color combination becomes workable in the hands of a skillful designer.

An example of a striking color combination used to produce depth on a two-dimensional plan is seen in the illustrated pendant. Even without the aid of a color illustration, the pendant demonstrates the designer's ability to create depth, movement and emotional involvement through color. The light-colored circular shape appears to open as a lens revealing diagonal lines and shapes which attract and

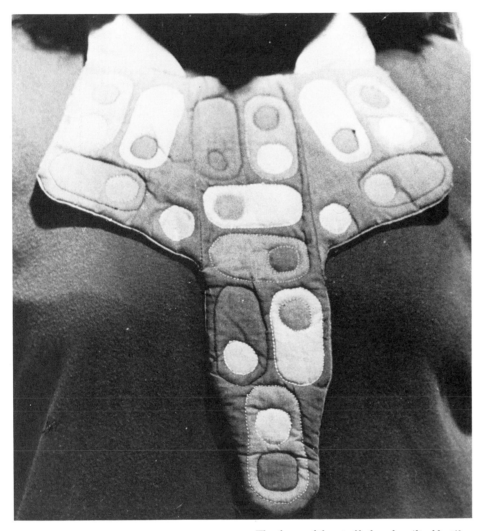

The form of the stuffed and quilted batik necklace compliments the human form for which it was created. Student artist, Oregon College of Education. Instructor, Ruth Culbertson.

move the eye. The dark rectangular shape surrounds and dramatizes the inner shapes adding to the illusion of depth.

Form

Form demands a unity of design purpose and places specific requirements on the soft jewelry designer. Viable, well-proportioned designs are built upon the aesthetic relationship of jewelry to the human form. For this reason, jewelry designed totally independent of the human subject often lacks functional validity.

Form also requires that there be continuity throughout an entire piece. This unity or integrity of design may be achieved in several different ways. One obvious method of gaining continuity is to repeat smaller design elements within the larger jewelry form. Another, more subtle method requires the designer to discover new but related forms that unify a design idea.

An illustration exemplifing unity of form can be seen in the quilted and stuffed batik necklace. The gentle curving lines of the external form are organic in nature, complimenting the human form. Internal continuity is achieved through stuffed and stitched molecular-like forms which relate to, but do not actually repeat, the external form.

Detail

Rhythm

Rhythm is the arrangement of design elements into progressive patterns which build visual movement through repetition. Rhythmic patterns in soft jewelry design are instrumental in affecting a mood and creating action. The eyes move easily over visual elements which are the same. This lack of variety invariably becomes monotonous, but is desirable in some situations. A uniform string of beads, for instance, does not distract from the impact of a more important component, the pendant.

In more complex designs, the use of line, shape, color and texture are combined to produce several different rhythmic patterns that exist simultaneously and harmoniously in the same composition.

This type of rhythmic progression can be seen in the woven collar with a bell. The inner circle of the collar appears to flow evenly around regular areas of color. The central portion of the collar is more lively with a varied progression of colored shapes. The outer circle of vibrant green and red vertical stripes around the exterior border of the collar build and intensify the rhythmic tempo.

Rhythmic patterns, combining color, shape and form are responsible for the visual excitement in this woven collar. Artist, Christena Weber.

58

Balance

Balance is the method by which elements of a design are ordered, enabling opposing forces in a composition to be equalized. Through balance, a feeling of "rightness" is achieved which is essential to the success of all design.

Symmetrical placement is the most direct and obvious way to balance a composition. Design elements are repeated in a mirror-like progression, so that a design using a bead on the upper right-hand corner will also place a bead at the upper left-hand corner.

Radial symmetrical balance is especially pertinent to the design of soft jewelry. Using the neck opening as the center axis, design elements radiate from this point with identical placement on either side of the circle.

Balance may also be achieved through asymmetrical placement. Asymmetrical balance equalizes opposing forces which are dissimilar in size, color, shape, pattern, texture and form but which become balanced by careful placement within the visual composition.

A symmetrical balance is present in the satin and silver collar with stitchery and beads. The placement of Mylar shapes is varied. Balance is accomplished by the creation of textural patterns of stitches and beads which equalize the visual weight of the diverse areas within the design.

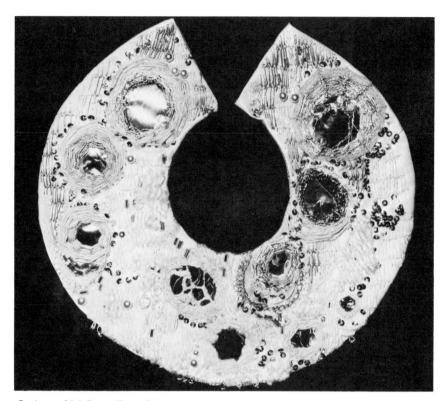

Satin and Mylar collar achieves an asymmetrical balance through textural details that equalize the visual importance of different areas. Artist, B. J. Adams.

Design Ideas

There are no set formulas by which a designer can discover visual inspiration. Visually stimulating materials exist everywhere. The ability to recognize design ideas present in nature and people-made environments is based on an individual's capacity to see and grasp images and impressions which are not apparent to the casual observer.

The ability to critically analyze what is perceived is present in varying degrees in all of us. However, it can be further enhanced by a conscious effort to focus attention on objects and images that might otherwise be overlooked. Our eyes, used in combination with other senses, enable us to assimilate an enormous storehouse of images upon which we can later draw.

By developing this awareness, the discovery of the design possibilities present in the visual world becomes self-generating. A flattened pull-top from a soft drink can may have remained unnoticed in the litter of a parking lot without the discerning eye of the designer who saw an intriguing shape and recognized the design possibilities. This discovery, which took only a moment to make, eventually grew into the stuffed and stitched necklace shown in the illustration.

Designs inspired by nature are as valid as those with more obscure beginnings. The designer must continue to reject solutions which are trite reproductions of nature.

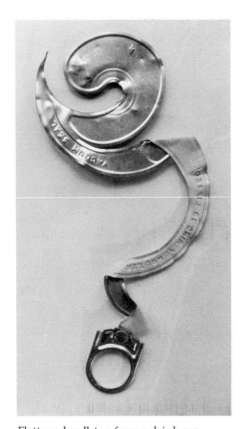

Flattened pull-top from a drink can.

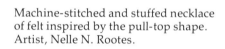

Machine-stitched and stuffed necklace of felt inspired by the pull-top shape. Artist, Nelle N. Rootes.

Detail

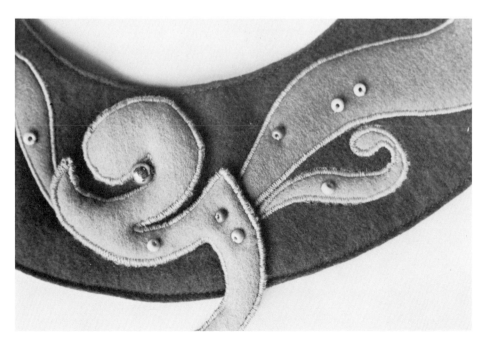

Sunflower

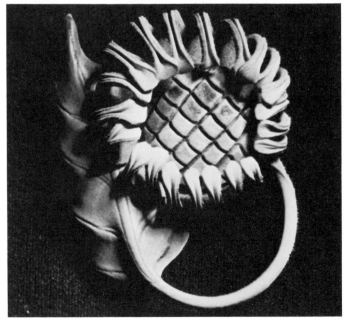

An artist's concept of a sunflower expressing the medium of molded leather. Artist, Daphne Lingwood.

Nature remains the original and most innovative designer. Natural materials viewed in purely an abstract sense are composed of line, color, space, form, texture, rhythm and balance, displaying nearly perfect design solutions. The ability to recognize the natural relationships of design elements and reassemble them into a personal design statement presents a challenge of the highest order.

Designs inspired by nature begin with an original source. As the designer investigates a single object, such as a flower, personal viewpoints begin to emerge. Every individual will see and experience the same object differently. One designer may portray the singularity of a particular flower. Another designer might prefer to select a single design element for exploration and develop it in a totally different direction or build a composition based on an abstraction of the flower. Yet another artist may represent the generalities of a certain variety of flowers with a stylized rendition.

The latter is illustrated in the sunflower pin of molded leather which captures a symbolic vision of a sunflower through stylized lines and patterns. The rhythm and symmetry relating to the actual flower are retained without sacrificing the artist's personal concept.

Colors used in weaving the fabric for this collar correspond to those present in the attached peacock feathers. Artist, Catherine Crossman.

Natural materials often inspire designs that are executed in other media. The object of inspiration may also be incorporated into the jewelry. The woven collar with peacock feathers is an example of this. The greens, blues and gold present in the eye of the feather were duplicated in the colorful patterns of the woven collar. The choice of color and its placement in the woven pattern serve to visually and emotionally link the two materials.

As shown, a single visual stimulus in the real world is capable of prompting a design idea which ultimately results in soft jewelry. However, design ideas rarely depend on a single factor, but rather develop as a culmination of diverse experiences.

Books and periodicals are an obvious and indispensable source for design ideas. Especially pertinent are those books depicting folk art, ancient jewelry and costumes which aid in familiarizing the designer with the concept of adornment.

More specific ideas may be derived by investigating the arts of a particular culture such as the American Indian or Black African. The bold uninhibited use of materials, attention to detail, complex geometric patterns and design symmetry are only a few of the inspirational qualities found in these works.

The African neckpiece from Tusti, Rwanda, is an ingenious use of available material. Made of goat skin covered in a pattern of black and white seed beads and fringed with the white hair of a Colobus monkey, the neckpiece is a striking example of the dynamic expression of another culture.

Design inspirations often come from an appreciation of jewelry of other cultures. This African neckpiece of goat skin, seed beads and hair from a Colobus monkey is from Tutsi, Rwanda. Photograph courtesy of UCLA Museum of Cultural History.

Personal Expressions

Multiple images and complex impressions that evoke a feeling or emotional response are equally important to design inspiration. The search for an appropriate medium for self-expression in soft jewelry can lead through many levels of adaptation as designs grow and take direction. To express a complex idea successfully, the designer is compelled to seek materials and methods relevant to the idea to be conveyed. This is accomplished through experimentation with a familiar medium, and frequently requires exploration of several alternative methods.

Girl With A Rainbow depends on the use of stitchery to draw a dream-like fantasy. The abstract landscape and figure derive their illusionary quality from a network of stitches. And although this technique was successful within the range of requirements set for the initial piece, the exclusive use of stitchery became a limiting factor for self-expression. In order to develop the illustrative concept found in *Girl With A Rainbow* even further, pen and ink drawings were applied on stitched and stuffed freeform fabric. By choosing a technique well suited to the production of details and fine lines, the illusory quality of the work was heightened. The resulting neckpiece, entitled *Faces*, represents one designer's solution in the search for individual expression.

The artist uses stitchery to create the dream-like fantasy of *Girl With A Rainbow*. Artist, Julie Fatherley.

Detail

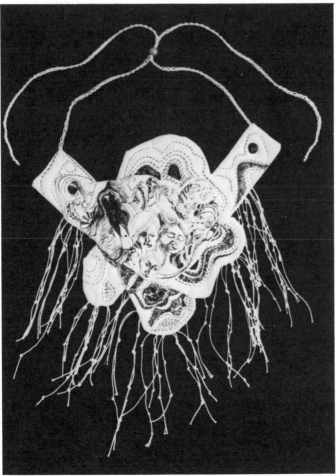

The neckpiece *Faces* combines pen and ink drawings with stitchery in a further refinement of the artist's expression. Artist, Julie Fatherley.

Chapter 4

Design and Construction Techniques

Proper construction techniques are essential to the success of soft jewelry, for it is here that the validity of the piece is established as materials are organized into a design.

Because of the broad range of soft materials available, it is virtually impossible to review each and every construction technique that might be encountered. However, there are general construction techniques such as cutting, stitching, bonding, knotting, wrapping, etc., which can be easily adapted to meet specific design requirements. This chapter is concerned with these techniques not as an end in themselves, but as they contribute to the process of designing soft jewelry.

Design Considerations in Jewelry Construction

Design and construction are interdependent and both must be considered throughout the entire working process. Construction methods and materials that are compatible will aid in unifying a design. Functional as well as decorative materials should be visually appropiate and consistent with the design intent. Complex construction methods do not necessarily insure design success. Designs that are overworked lose their identity. The most effective construction techniques are often those that are the least obvious for they have become an inseparable part of the total design concept.

Artist, Virginia I. Harvey

Two very professionally executed macramé necklaces use essentially the same knot for construction, yet make very different design statements.

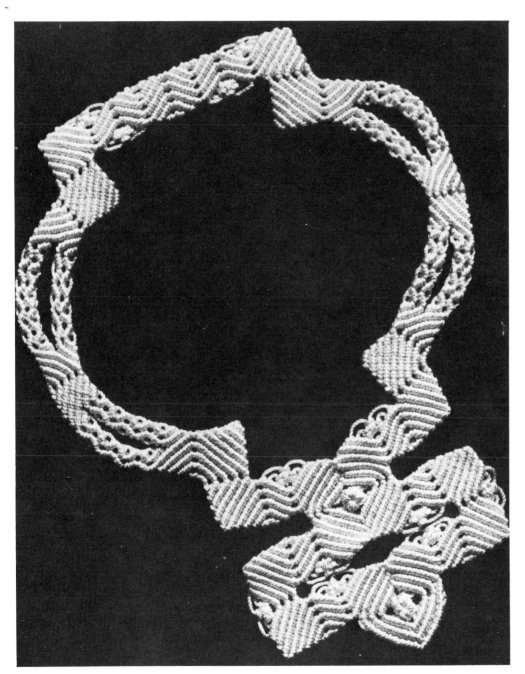

Artist, Joan Michaels-Paque

Cutting

Suggested materials and methods:

Material	*Cutting Method*
fiber and fabric	scissors
leather	scissors, matte knife, punch
polystyrene	matte knife, hack saw
plastic vinyls	scissors
dried natural materials	scissors, matte knife
feathers	scissors
bone	power saw, hack saw
shells	power saw, drill, hack saw
found metal	hack saw
found glass	glass cutter

Cutting Leather:

(a) Pattern is drawn on leather with pointed punch.

(b) Pattern is cut from leather with utility knife.

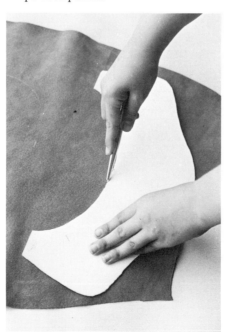

Piercing and Punching

Piercing and punching are methods used to further prepare materials for assembly.

Piercing creates holes through which string, wire or other fasteners can be inserted. A sharp awl or hand drill is usually satisfactory for piercing. But in the case of fragile materials such as Styrofoam, papier-mâché or feathers, a power drill is recommended.

Punches are available in different sizes and shapes and are most often associated with leather working. Inexpensive general purpose punches found in hardware stores are adequate for punching holes into cardboard, heavy fabric and polystyrene. A specialized leather punch, the rotating punch, will be needed to create holes for lacing. Leather punches can also be used with heavy vinyl as well as with different grades of leather.

Stringing

For thousands of years, man has created jewelry by stringing combinations of interesting and beautiful materials to create rhythmic patterns in design and color. Stringing is a method in which separate elements are chosen and interrelated as they are positioned on the string.

The type of string used will be determined by the size and shape of the beads or elements and the pattern desired. Heavy nylon fishing line may be ideal for large beads with small holes; however, every-

thing from leather thongs to dental floss can be used for stringing.

The simplest method of stringing fits one bead tightly against its neighbor, omitting intervening spaces and inviting the eye to follow the strung material without interruption. Another stringing method allows for space between each separate element to attract or trick the eye. Compare the knotted separations between each element in the crocheted string of pearls with those knotted separations found in the macramé medallion necklace. The knots which accent the beads of the crocheted pearls are essential to the feeling of the design. The knots separate and emphasize the bead-like quality of each element. In the

Basket of Pearls, crocheted creation with stuffed beads, features a container in a contrasting color. Artist, Renie Breskin Adams.

second example, knots are used as space. The beads, knots and cord have been combined into a form in which they lose their separate identities. These examples point out the importance of separation as well as organization.

Finally, there is the problem of stringing one single element, such as a pendant. Here the material will be chosen in accordance with the requirements of the pendant. Functionally, the material must support the element. Aesthetically, the material should allow the main focus of attention to rest on the single design element. Materials used within a pendant can be repeated in the stringing medium. A metallic cord might hold a metallic pendant of stitchery. Or a totally different material, which has some subtle relationship either to color or pattern in the pendant, may be an effective stringing material.

Medallion Necklace of waxed linen cord, wooden beads and ring. Artist, Sharon Paulsen.

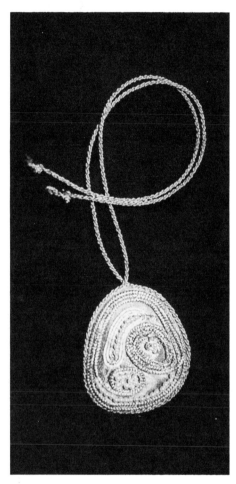

Stitched pendant with metal thread and pearls. Artist, Bucky King.

Machine embroidered pendant with beads. Artist, Lynn Bassler.

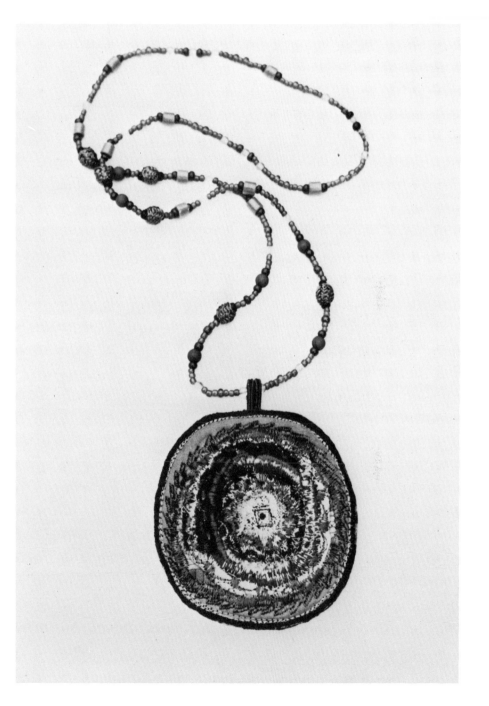

Stitching

Stitched construction in soft jewelry is multifaceted. Both hand and machine stitching can be used, and in many cases, both will be necessary in the design and construction of a single piece.

Three-dimensional fabric forms for soft jewelry are usually constructed from two pieces of fabric secured with machine stitching and later stuffed.

Stitched construction begins with a cardboard pattern of the jewelry shape to be created. The cardboard shape is placed on the reverse side of a piece of fabric and a pencil outline is drawn. Now the second square of fabric is pinned to the first piece with the front sides together. The fabric is then stitched along the pencil line, leaving an open space to allow for stuffing. Excess material is trimmed away around the seam of the stitched shape. The fabric shape is turned right side out and stuffed. When stuffing has been completed, the open edge is finished with blind stitching.

This particular stitched and stuffed form has been prepared with a wrapped end in order that it may be combined into a necklace of multiple forms. An example of this technique can be seen in the illustrated necklace composed of heart-shaped forms.

Creating stitched and stuffed forms:

(a) Pattern of shape is traced onto fabric.
(b) Machine stitched shape with open space for inserting stuffing.
(c) Excess fabric is trimmed from stitched seam.
(d) Stuffing is inserted after fabric has been turned right side out.
(e) Blind stitching is used to finish seam.
(f) Finished stuffed form with wrapped end.

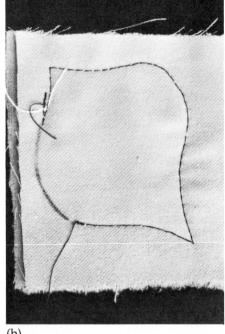

(b)

(a)

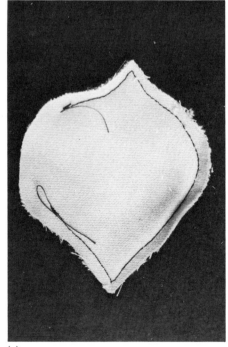

(c)

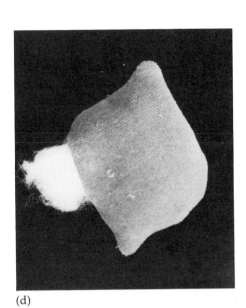

(d)

(f)

Necklace composed of heart-shaped, stuffed forms. Artist, Lucretia Romey.

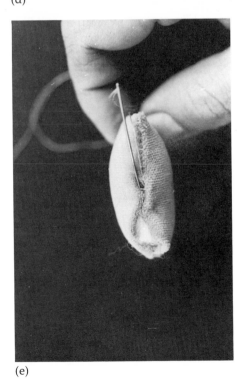

(e)

Stitched and stuffed necklace created from bleached black cotton. Artist, Betty Ruth Curtiss. Photograph by Cliff Moore.

In an example with a very different feeling, three large stuffed forms dominate the necklace. Selectively bleached black cotton fabric was used to create the large forms joined with hand stitching around a neckband. A found metal ring bound in the center completes the design.

Weaving

Weaving is a basic technique in the design and construction of soft jewelry. Because woven jewelry is relatively small, the creation of freeform woven shapes for jewelry challenges the seasoned weaver as well as the novice.

The only requirement in making a workable loom for jewelry is that the warp must be stretched to provide tension in order that the weft can run over and under the single fibers of warp.

There are several different approaches to loom construction for jewelry weaving. The board loom, frame loom and the back strap loom are all usable, but the simplest, most successful looms for weaving irregular shapes are those made from cardboard, poster board or bristol board. Corrugated cardboard is not recommended.

The shape of the loom will depend upon the shape desired in the final weaving. Looms for woven collars and neckpieces might be oval, oblong, or round according to the design planned. Looms for bracelets are often rectangular, with the length of the cardboard cut to the

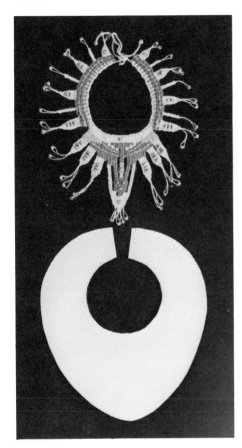

Oval cardboard loom was used to produce woven collar.

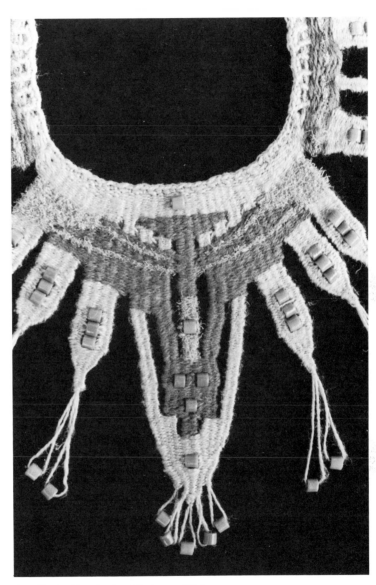

Detail of collar. Artist, Christena Weber.

circumference of the wrist. There are a number of shapes which will work equally well. The oval cardboard loom, on which the woven collar illustrated was produced, is one possible shape.

Loom construction begins by drawing the exterior shape of the loom on a piece of heavy cardboard. The circular loom (shown) began with a circle 13 inches in diameter. Next a point on the circle is marked to indicate center back. A ruler is placed at this point and a mark is made two inches inside the circle from the center back. This mark indicates the placement of the second circle, which is 6½ inches in diameter and will become the neck hole. Two slightly angled lines are placed about ¾'' from the center back to allow for the back opening in the woven piece. Using the compass to measure, marks are made every ⅛'' around the circumference of the small circle. Now a pin is placed at the axis of the neck hole circle. The placement of notches on the exterior circle is determined by resting the edge of the ruler against the center axis pin across the mark made on the interior circle. There will be one mark placed on the exterior circle for each mark on the interior circle. After marking is completed, the loom may be cut and notched with heavy scissors or a matte knife.

In order to warp the cardboard loom, the first warp thread is tied at the back of the loom. The thread is then pulled around the first notch

and across the loom to the matching notch on the exterior circle.

This particular loom has been double warped, enabling the weaver to create an intricate color pattern. Another special feature of this warp are the bells and beads positioned just behind each notch on the exterior circle. Bells and beads were threaded onto the warp to serve as finishing for the warp ends and to help hold weaving tension taut as work progresses.

Making a cardboard loom:

(a) A ruler is placed at the center back. A mark is made two inches inside large circle to indicate the placement of neck hole opening.

(b) A smaller circle is drawn for neck hole openings.

(c) Using the center of the neck hole opening as an axis point, a ruler is used to mark the exterior circle with notches which correspond to those marked on the interior circle.

(d) Warping a cardboard loom. (front view)

(e) Back view of warped loom indicates placement of beads and bells.

(f) Partially completed woven collar.

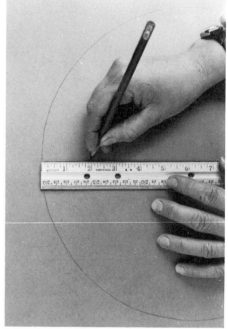

(a)

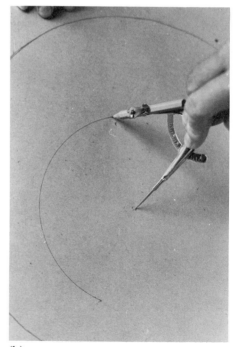

(b)

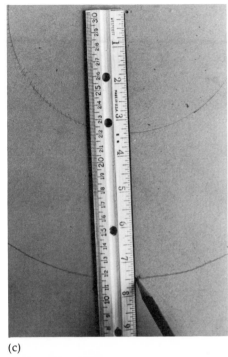

(c)

(e)

(d)

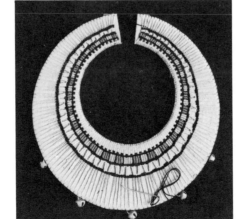

(f)

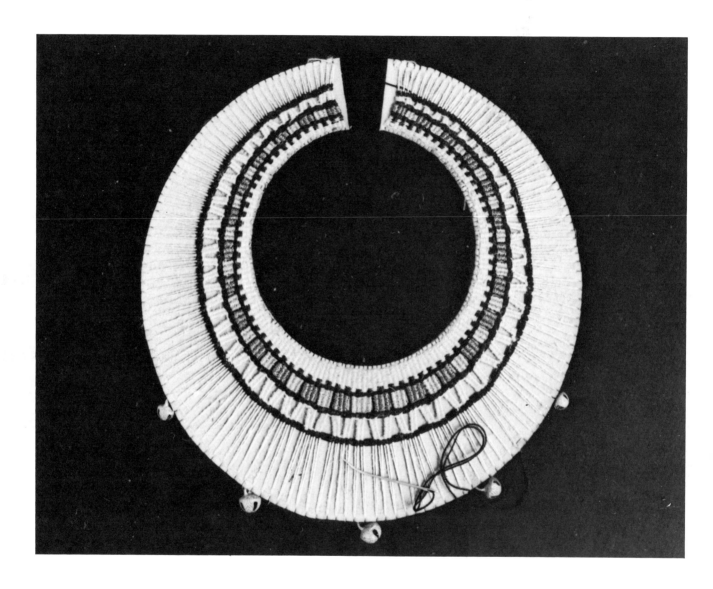

Following warping, weaving can begin. A curved sacking needle threaded with weft is excellent for weaving on a cardboard loom, since it allows the weaver to weave in and out without stretching the warp.

After the weaving has been completed and removed from the loom, a piece of cord or yarn is inserted though the warp ends, around the neck opening and tied in the back to finish the collar.

This woven design, inspired by the ancient Egyptian collars, is built around jewel-like patterns of color dramatized by the use of a slit tapestry technique. The circular shape of the loom has influenced the designs but not restricted the shape of the finished piece.

Woven collar removed from the loom.
Artist, Christina Weber.

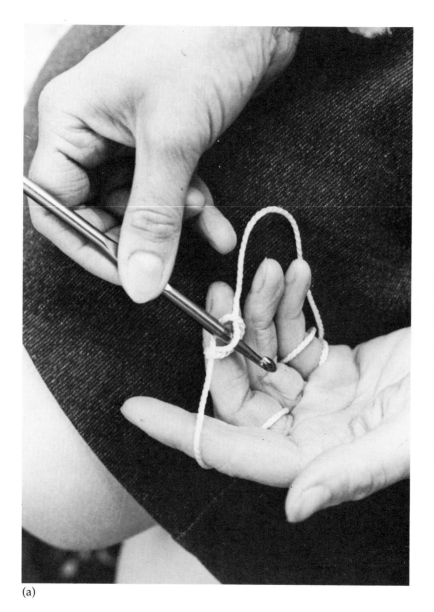

(a)

Crocheting

Crochet is another needleworking technique that may be used for making soft jewelry. Basic stitches are easily mastered and, from this foundation, the designer has an almost inexhaustible number of variations with which to improvise. Self-contained three-dimensional forms, stuffed forms, delicate lacey patterns and surface textures are all attainable in crocheted jewelry designs.

Crocheting begins with a slip knot and progresses into chains of stitches. This is accomplished by pulling one loop through another with the aid of a crochet hook. The simple chain stitch becomes the basis of other more complex stitches around which crochet patterns are built. Double crochet is a basic stitch commonly combined with the chain to form a simple crocheted pattern. Another versatile stitch, the single crochet, is excellent for finishing edges on both woven and crocheted jewelry.

Basic crochet stitches:

(a) Crocheting begins with a slip knot.

(b) Chain stitch is created by passing hook under yarn, catching yarn with hook, and drawing it through loop.

(c) Double crochet stitch.

(d) Single crochet stitch is used to finish edge.

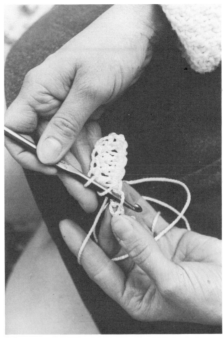

(c)

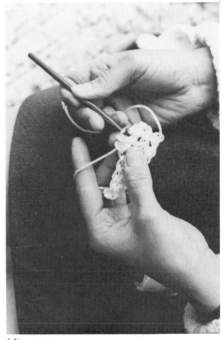

(d)

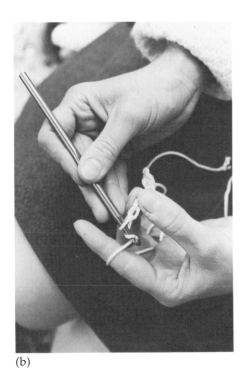

(b)

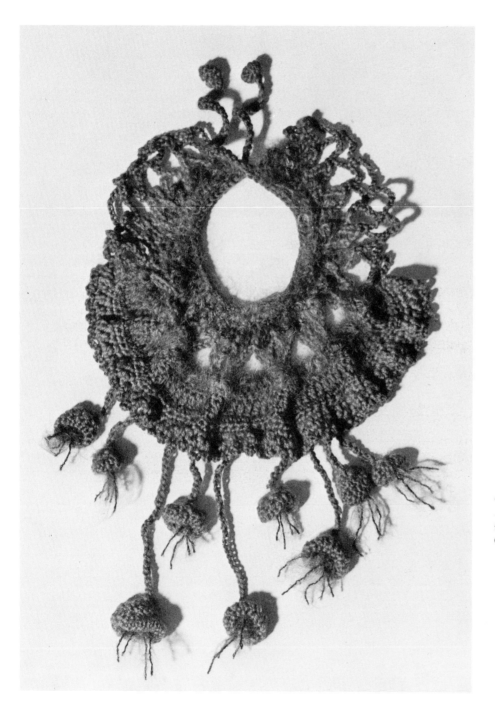

When designing crocheted jewelry keep in mind that the crochet stitches are only a means to an end and need not dominate the work. The crochet necklace of wool and mohair illustrates this point. The crochet stitches used in the construction of the necklace are secondary to the designer's involvement with fiber in the creation of texture and motion.

A quite different design approach can be seen in the collar created from a unique combination of brass wire and linen fiber. Stitches are crocheted in delicate patterns providing a positive visual contribution to the design. Different in feeling from the crocheted necklace, which is more fluid in quality, the collar exhibits an elegance borne out of symmetry of line, pattern and color.

Crocheted necklace of red-, magenta-, and rust-colored wool and mohair. Artist, Dolly Curtis. Photograph by Victor Cromwell.

Crocheted brass wire and linen necklace
with beads. Artist, Bucky King. Photograph by W. S. King.

Knotting

Macramé or knotting techniques for soft jewelry are relatively simple to master. Knotting requires no specialized tools and affords the designer an opportunity to create spontaneously — even with a limited repertoire of knots.

Usually, well designed macramé jewelry depends upon skillful variations of basic knots, rather than complex knotting. For instance, the basic square knot can take many forms: used as a single knot for fastening, the square knot becomes ornamental; tied in alternating rows, the square knot exhibits an overall textured pattern; or when tied consecutively around core cords, the square knot creates a three-dimensional sinnet.

The macramé necklace with bells is one example of a design created almost entirely of square knot sinnets. The necklace took shape originally as five separate pastel-colored sinnets, each tied to a length of one inch. Sinnets were then joined by tying a square knot in the adjacent cords. The sinnet knotting is resumed for an additional inch-and-one-half before the sinnets are joined again for the second time. Sinnets are then knotted an additional length of two-and-one-half inches and finished by attaching ornamental bells.

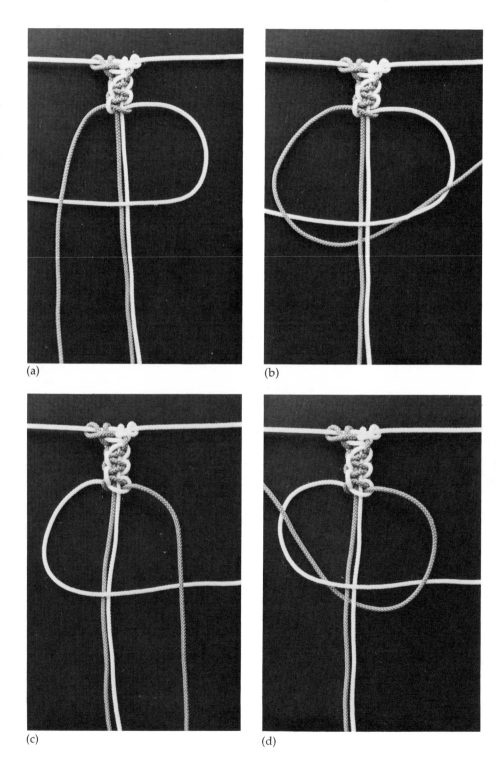

(a)

(b)

(c)

(d)

86

Tying square knot sinnet:

(a) Square knot is composed of two separate knots. The first knot is tied by passing the white cord at the right over the pair in the center and under the dark cord.

(b) The dark cord at the left is then passed under the pair at the center and through the loop made by the white cord.

(c) The second half of the knot is tied by passing the white cord, now on the left over the pair at the center and under the dark cord on the right.

(d) The knot is completed by passing the dark cord at the right under the pair at the center and through the loop made by the white cord. Pull taut.

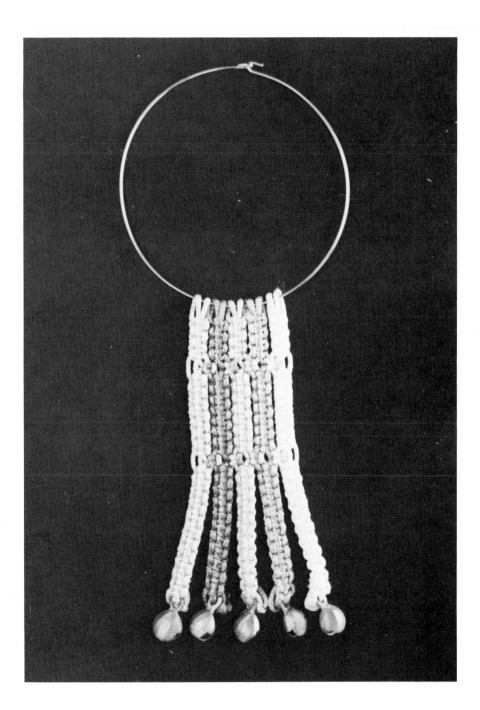

Macramé necklace composed of square knot sinnets. Artist, Roxanne Kukuk.

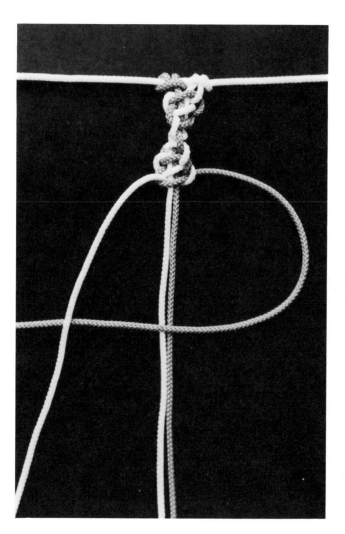

Another basic knot, the half knot, also has many forms. The half knot is created by tying a slight variation of the square knot. Spiral sinnets are produced by tying the first half of the square knot sequence consecutively around core cords. (See illustration).

An effective use of the half knot sinnet is seen in the macramé necklace with beads. The necklace is composed of three separate half knot sinnets joined at the center back and again at the center front. Carefully proportioned sinnets of varying lengths were used to produce the interior pattern of the necklace. The sinnets were finished by threading integrated cords through natural colored beads. To complete the necklace the cords were tied and fringed.

A half knot sinnet is formed when only the first half of the square knot is repeated.

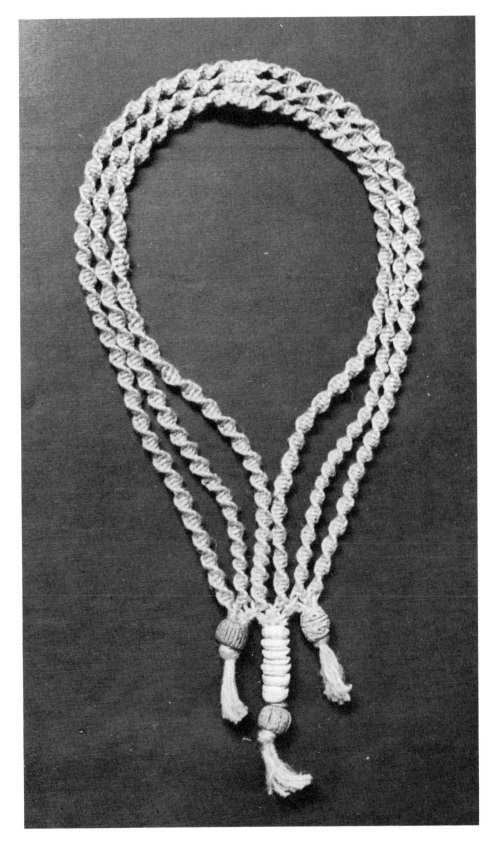

Necklace composed of half knot sinnets.
Artist, Pat Fosnaught.

Wrapping

Wrapping has long been a finishing technique to secure warp ends or to create tassels in woven and knotted creations. However, in addition, wrapping is an outstanding technique for soft jewelry because it follows the shape of a variety of core materials, while exhibiting unique textures of its own.

The design and construction of wrapped jewelry begins with a core of material around which yarn, cord or thread is wrapped. Core material might be a single rope, many small cords, fabric strips, plastic tubing or any other imaginable material. The primary demand is that the wrapping be applied evenly and that color changes be made without surface distortions.

One simple wrapping technique uses a tapestry needle to secure the wrapped cord ends. Wrapping begins by placing the wrapping cord alongside the core material. The single cord is then coiled over itself and wrapped upward around the core. When wrapping has been completed, or when the wrapping cord becomes short, a tapestry needle is placed into the wrapped coil. The wrapping cord is fed through the needle and the needle is then pulled back through the wrapped coil. Any excess may then be trimmed.

The wrapped necklace of multicolored wools began with a core of sisal rope. The curving form of the rope helped to control the shape of the jewelry. Shapes were created

when portions of the rope were joined with a figure eight wrapping. Anchor cords were added to hold the wrapped shapes in place and create variety in the overall pattern.

Wrapping:

(a) Wrapping cord is placed alongside core material.

(b) Yarn is wrapped around core of sisal rope.

(c) Needle is inserted into coil. Yarn is threaded through needle and pulled back through wrapping to secure end.

(b)

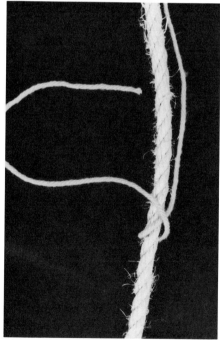

(a)

(c)

Multicolored wrapped necklace formed around a core of sisal rope. Artist, Julie Fatherley.

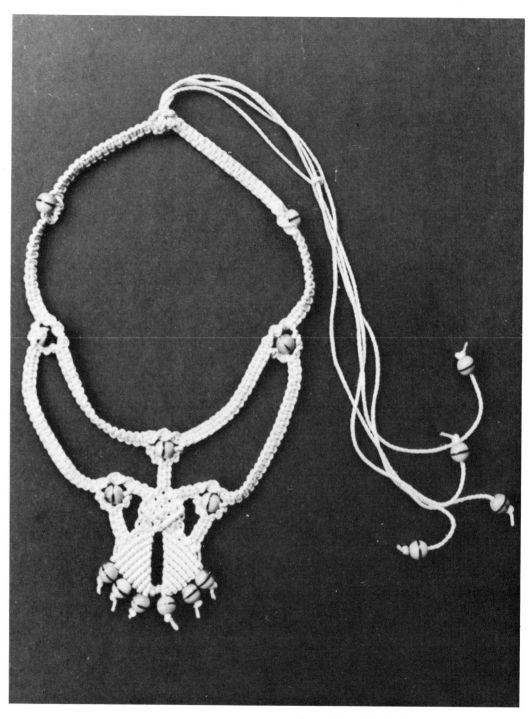

Inventive slipknot fastening contributes to the success of macramé necklace design. Artist, Judy Hollanger.

Fastening

Fastening one material to another or a material to itself has always been a major concern of jewelry designers. Soft jewelry is no exception. The options are numerous. Soft jewelry elements can be strung, sewn, bonded or created in one continuous piece. They might be fastened with jump rings as in metal jewelry or simply wrapped and tied. Although the techniques are not complex and can be easily mastered, the success of any single fastening will depend upon the appropriateness of the material and fulfillment of its function within the design.

Let us consider several fastening alternatives as they relate to various materials and methods. For example, a clear drying glue which bonds surfaces is purely functional. The fastening material does not change the visual impact of the design. However, an entirely different type of fastening solution, the metal jump ring, must be dealt with on a visual as well as a functional level. Jump rings not only fasten, they create a feeling of space within the design. They are used to isolate or incorporate other materials even though they remain subordinate.

Still another solution integrates the fastening technique with the design material. An example can be seen in the woven wool neckpiece incorporating separate woven units with wrapping. The line, color and pattern of the wrapped portion of the neckpieces has been integrated with the woven portion. They have been successfully combined into a unified creation.

Wrapping was used to combine soft woven elements into neckpiece. Student artist, Oregon College of Education. Instructor, Ruth Culbertson.

Bonding and Gluing

When materials are adhered more or less permanently, they are said to be bonded. Bonding allows for interesting combinations of both color and texture and can be a practical technique for jewelry construction.

Modern technology has supplied us with a large variety of bonding products and glues created for special industrial bonding problems. They are strong, durable and allow for adhesion between materials previously impossible to bond. The strongest of these are the epoxy resins consisting of two parts; one of which is the hardening agent that is mixed into the glue just before it is applied. Gray-colored epoxy paste is ideal for bonding jewelry findings that might otherwise require soldering. Clear drying epoxy glues are useful for joining some types of soft plastic.

Other clear drying household glue is fine for paper, polystryene, fiber and porous materials. Vinyl and leather may be bonded with contact cement. And one of the most useful products for constructing soft jewelry is the heat sensitive bonding sheets which can be placed between layers of fabric and pressed with an iron, causing the fabric to be joined as one.

Woven necklace with central medallion bonded to wood. Artist, Catherine Crossman. Photography by Walt Peterson.

94

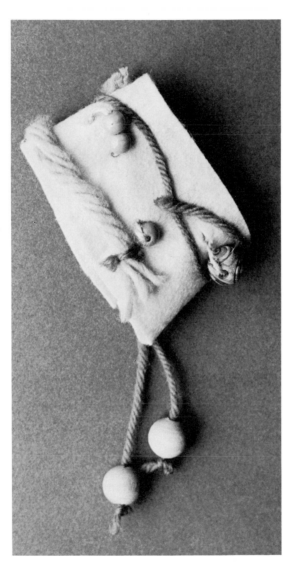

Beads and yarn tied onto felt bracelet.
Student, grade 5.

Tying

From the simplest hitch to the most complex macramé knot, tying can incorporate materials that might not otherwise be combined. Pliable materials such as fiber, cord, plastic tubing, leather thongs, metallic thread and soft metal wire can all be fastened to themselves or to other materials by tying.

The simplest form of tying merely attaches one material to another. The knots are functional and should be chosen for their strengh and longevity. Square knots are perfect for this use. (See Knotting).

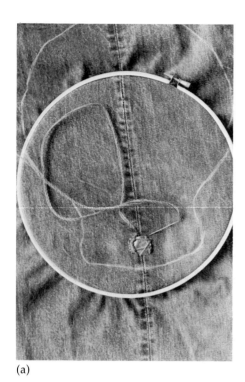

(a)

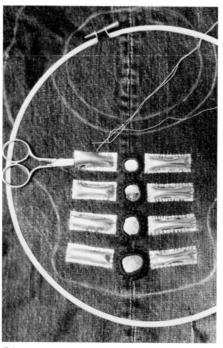

(b)

Stitching

Most fabric jewelry requires some form of stitching as a means of fastening one material to another. These include both machine and hand stitching to apply materials and shapes to the surface of the primary fabric design.

One method of fastening decorative materials to a background fabric is illustrated in the *Denim Collar*. The fabric was first pulled taut with an embroidery hoop. Bits of tiny mirrors were enclosed in stitches of blue yarn. The stuffed rectangles of silver Mylar were then stitched in place with thread. The stitches used for this application are visible and contribute a decorative quality of their own.

In another example, a body contour necklace, machine stitching was used exclusively. Stitching holds the elements of batik fabric in place while it visually separates and defines form within the stuffed fabric. Here the method of construction is not decorative in itself, but contributes greatly to the visual success of the design.

Attaching materials with stitches:

(a) After an outline of the jewelry design is drawn on the fabric with chalk, the fabric is placed in an embroidery hoop. The first tiny mirror is encased within a network of four stitches over which decorative stitches are applied.

(b) Each rectangle of silver Mylar is stuffed and stitched to the fabric with thread. Small scissors aid in holding stuffing in place while stitching is in progress.

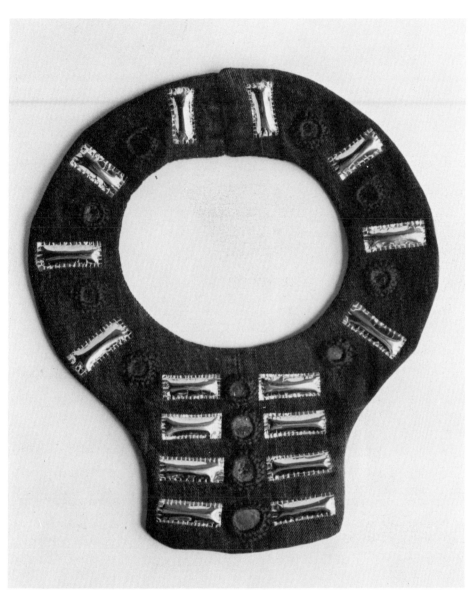

Completed *Denim Collar*. Artist, Roxanne Kukuk.

Stitched and stuffed fabric collage necklace with batik accents. Student artist, Oregon College of Education. Instructor, Ruth Culbertson.

Creating Findings

Almost all jewelry requires functional findings that allow the wearer to fasten and remove the adornment. Jewelry findings must be practical, attractive and workable over a long period of time. They should be well crafted and visually integrated within the total jewelry design.

An obvious solution to the problem of findings might be to create jewelry which needs no fastening device. Findings are not needed for necklaces that fit over the head or bracelets that slip on and off the wrist.

However, the designer who wishes to avoid the problem of findings will discover it is not possible in all cases. Findings are an indispensable part of almost every jewelry design.

When determining an approach to findings, use the most direct method available. Consider using the materials from which the jewelry is being constructed. Materials that can be tied, bent or twisted into fasteners will need only slight alteration in order to make them wearable. A decorative knot tied into a leather thong or a macramé cord that can be quickly tied and re-tied for successive wearings are examples of design materials converted into self-fasteners. Other cords with less strength might be adapted into fasteners by knotting a loop at one end which attaches to a knotted button or bead at the other end. Wire chokers may be fastened

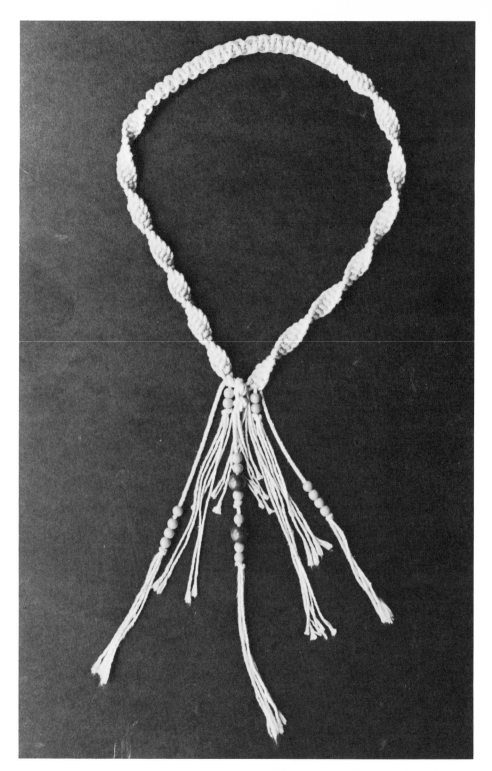

Necklace of square knots and half knot sinnets was designed to slip over the head. Student, grade 8.

98

Button and loop fasteners were knotted to finish macramé necklace. Artist, Joan Michaels-Paque.

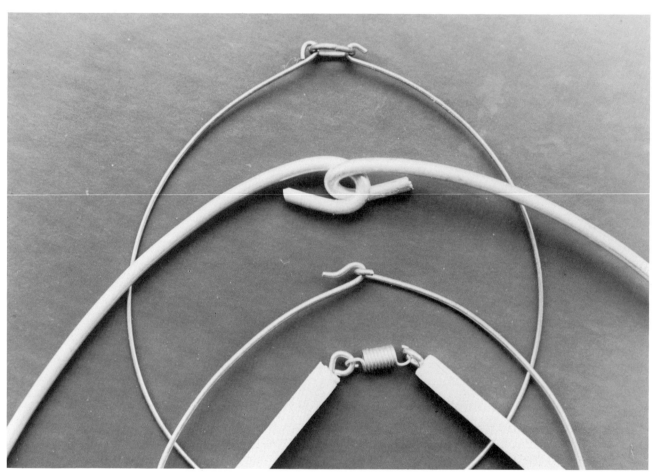

Fasteners featuring "hook-to-hook" and "hook-and-eye" configurations.

by simply bending both ends into a "hook-to-hook" or "hook-and-eye" configuration.

Another common solution is to buy commercial findings. Pin backs, bracelets, clamps and earring wires are available in gold and silver finishes and are ideal for complex construction problems such as cuff link backs. Since commercial findings were originally intended for use on metal jewelry, they may not always be workable for "soft" designs. Buttons, hooks and eyes, snaps, zippers and other sewing products used for fastening garments provide an alternative to commercial findings. Finally, when none of the usual methods succeeds, explore original possibilities. Simple solutions for findings can be found in hardware stores. Screw-eyes, springs, clamps, clip hooks for dog chains, plastic curtain rings, plastic washers are only a few of the many manufactured materials that can be adapted into functional findings for jewelry.

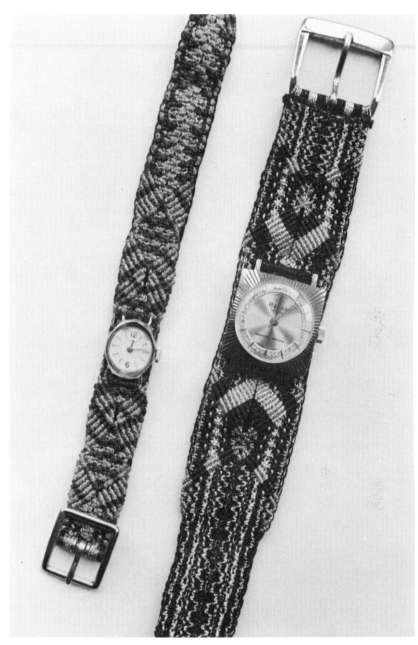

The functional demands of a wristwatch make commercial findings essential on these macramé bands. Artist, Judy Hollanger.

Chapter 5

Techniques For Further Exploration

As design ideas for soft jewelry begin to materialize, techniques often stabilize and become repetitious. To avoid this pitfall, several innovative methods for design and construction are covered in this final chapter. Each method is a favorite of the artist, teacher or craftsperson who created the work. It is hoped that through their insights and techniques, as well as through ideas gained from work already accomplished, new inroads can be made toward individual expression. Exploration of soft jewelry techniques is only just beginning!

Wire Weaving

Wire weaving is another off-loom technique with practical application for soft jewelry, but unlike most forms of off-loom jewelry, the actual weaving frame is retained in the final design.

Many types of wire, including jewelry wire, are usable for woven wire designs. The best choice will be one which contributes most to the design, both visually and structurally. This means that a wire which is easily bent by hand will be too soft, while heavy gauge wire may be too thick in diameter to be aesthetically pleasing in a small piece of jewelry.

A 14-gauge brass wire is used in this example. Brass, copper and silver wires are all attractive for jewelry, although they will require a fixative to prevent tarnishing.

The first step is to bend the wire into a shape that will eventually accommodate weaving. Jewelry or metal working tools are handy in this instance, but needle-nose pliers for bending and cutting wire is the only essential tool.

In the example, the wire has been bent into a circle by coiling. There are many other possibilities and several should be tried. Next, the wire extending from the top of the circle is formed into a fastening hook and fine wire is used to secure the first and second wires in order to stabilize the frame. Fine gauge copper wire is then interlaced into the body of the frame to create the warp through which the yarn weft is woven.

The next step is optional. Here, metal soldering is used to refine the frame before weaving. The first and second wires are joined permanently and a metal ring is added for fastening the pendant. It should also be noted that soldering allows small pieces of wire to be joined, making more complex structures possible.

After the secondary copper wire is in place and the soldering completed, weaving is begun on the outer circle of the frame. The weaving method may vary with the configuration of the frame and the fibers used, but usually a blunt tapestry or rounded upholstery needle will perform this function.

The second inter-structure of wire was added only after the outer portion of the circle was filled with yarn

Wire weaving:

(a) Brass wire formed into a pendant shape.

(b) Fine gauge wire is used to create an interstructure for weaving.

(c) First section of weaving is completed before second interstructure is added.

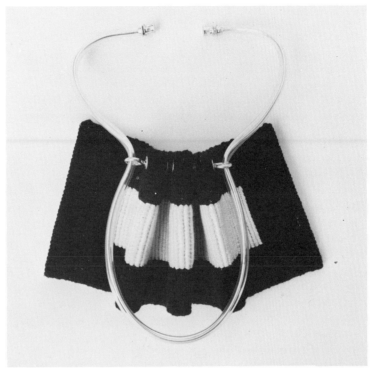

Knotted tapestry neckpiece. Artist, the author.

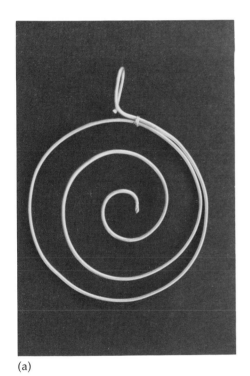

(a)

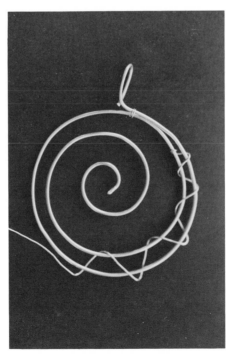

(b)

(c)

and the design idea evaluated. In the finished work, the space around the woven portion of the pendant, with its exposed structure of wire, is as important to the design statement as the solid areas of weaving.

A totally different feeling is conveyed by the solidly woven oval pendant. The shiny mass of melted brass attached near the center of the piece establishes a freeform shape around which the yarns flow, gradually enclosing the space inside the oval. Color variations are also important to the feeling of movement throughout the piece.

Hand formed brass wire chain is attached to the completed pendant. Artist, Kee Barbulesco. (actual size 2½″)

Oval pendant features multicolored yarns and free-form melted brass. Artist, Kee Barbulesco.

Needlepoint Embroidery

Creating needlepoint jewelry can be a surprisingly productive experience. Because the areas to be worked are usually small, making multiple color changes unnecessary, needlepoint jewelry encourages great flexibility. Individual discovery replaces detailed pre-planning as a design develops on the canvas.

Materials used in needlepoint are stocked in numerous stores. Crewel wool, Persian wool, tapestry wool and many other long, smooth fibers are all suitable for needlepoint jewelry. Needlepoint, or embroidery, canvas is available in several styles and mesh sizes. It is chosen in accordance with the area of the design planned. Single woven or mono canvas is easily worked and best for beginners. Remember, the mesh size controls the size of the stitches. Individual stitches should remain in correct proportion to the scale of the finished work. This suggests that a small piece of jewelry is more effective when created on canvas with small mesh openings. A #14 medium mesh was used for the illustrated pendant.

Usually the size of the tapestry needle is determined after the canvas mesh is chosen. The eye of the needle must be large enough to carry the yarn without stretching the mesh openings.

To calculate the amount of canvas needed, approximate the size of the finished piece and add one or two inches in all directions for a border or finishing allowance. Since jewelry designs will require only a portion of a regular canvas width, masking tape should be applied to all cut edges to prevent fraying while the needlepoint is being worked.

Designs for needlepoint often begin on graph paper, although it is not essential for small, simple jewelry. The actual canvas may be marked if color changes and stitch variations need to be indicated. Only indelible marking pens are suitable for this purpose. Canvas which is later worked with white yarn should not be marked.

In the illustrated example the first step is to establish the center of the rectangle of canvas by folding the piece into quarters. Tiny mirrors are then embroidered into place on either side of the center axis designated by the fold. (See illustration P. 96, (a), for embroidery stitch.) Next, a border of double leviathan needlepoint stitches is worked around the mirrors. Tiny beads are strung on individual loops as they are worked into the space between the mirrors and the border. Finally, the background is filled with the basket weave stitch. The needlepoint is now ready for blocking.

The method used to block needlepoint depends upon the desired final shape. Needlepoint which will remain flat should be mounted on a flat surface such as soft fiberboard that has been covered with wax paper. Before mounting, the completed canvas is evenly dampened with cold water. The damp needlepoint is then tacked to the board with push pins, while even tension is applied to all edges to insure even blockage.

After the canvas is dry, the needlepoint is ready for finishing. The outside edges of the illustrated pendant are bound with the binding stitch. Straps for mounting were worked and stitched to the back of

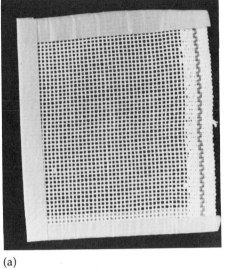

(a)

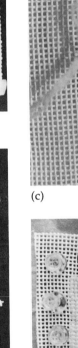

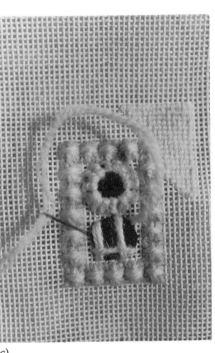

(c)

(b)

(d)

(e)

Needlepoint embroidery:

(a) Rectangle of #14 mono mesh canvas is masked ready for working.

(b) Tiny mirrors are positioned on either side of the center axis designated by the fold.

(c) Partially completed pendant illustrates various needlepoint and embroidery stitches used in construction.

(d) Completed canvas is blocked by mounting on soft fiberboard with push pins.

(e) Outside edge of the pendant is bound with a binding stitch.

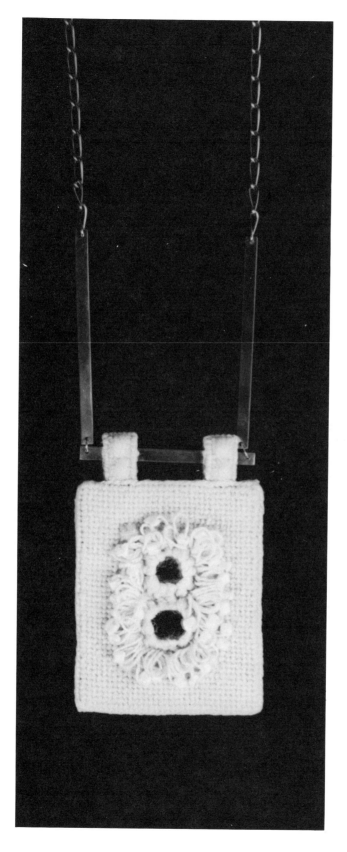

the main canvas. Lastly, in keeping with the elegance of the needlepoint design, the pendant was lined with white linen and hung from an especially created silver fastening.

Imaginative finishing solutions produce a variety of jewelry forms. The needlepoint pin shown is backed with felt to which a commercial pin finding is stitched. Still smaller canvases could be mounted on earring wires. Or, old plastic or metal bracelets might supply the frame for a needlepoint covering.

Especially created silver fastening holds the completed pendant. Artist, Roxanne Kukuk.

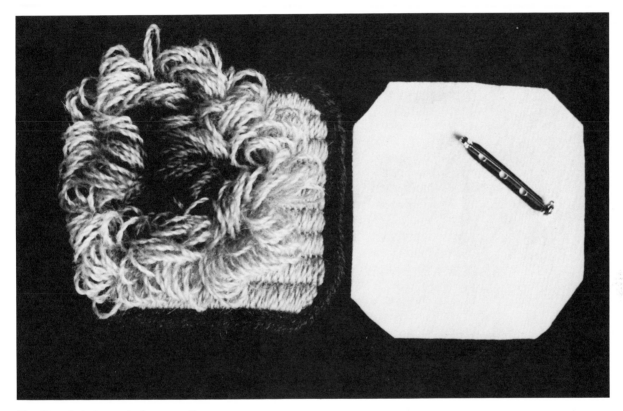

Needlepoint pin ready for mounting.
Artist, Roxanne Kukuk.

Coiled Basketry

Coiled basketry is a very old technique with many new applications. Soft jewelry design is one of the most intriguing expressions of this recent revival.

Coiled basketry is composed of two separate elements — the core which gives the work body and the external wrapping which supplies color and texture. The core material should be somewhat flexible, enabling the coil to be formed. The weft or yarn wrapping must be pliable but strong enough to join the coils without fraying. Remember, materials need to be compatible as well as functionally correct. Choose the core and weft as one design unit. Experiment until a workable combination is found.

To begin a coil, cut the core at an angle to produce a tapered end. Thread a blunt tapestry needle with yarn. This is the wrapping material or weft. Position the end of the weft approximately two inches from the end of the core. Wrap the weft over itself leaving the tapered end of the core exposed. After covering approximately an inch of core, bend the tapered end into a circle and continue wrapping over both the core and the end. Bring the needle through the hole formed by wrapping. After the circle is completed, begin a second coil by again wrapping the core for several turns. The second row is then secured to the first coil with the figure eight stitch.

Coiled basketry:

(a) Weft is positioned approximately two inches from the tapered end of the core.

(b) Weft is wrapped over itself leaving the tapered core exposed.

(c) After approximately an inch of core is wrapped, the tapered end is bent into a circle and wrapped.

(d) The needle is brought through the hole formed by wrapping.

(e) A second row is begun after the circle has been completed.

(f) The second row is then secured to the first coil with the figure eight or Navajo stitch. Photographs by Clark G. Adams.

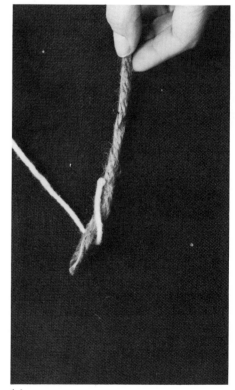

(a)

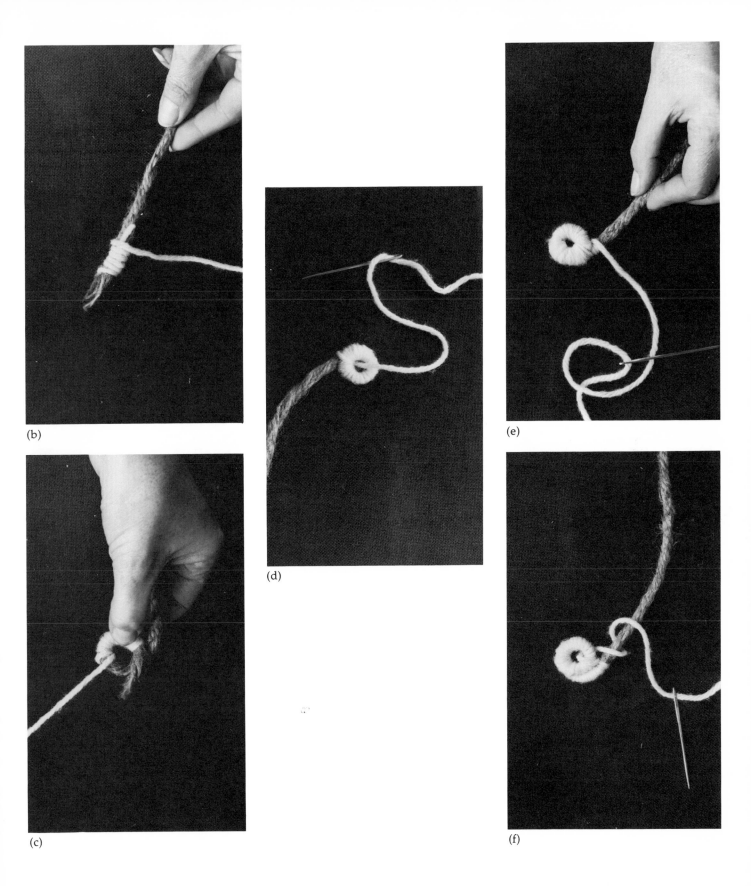

(b)

(c)

(d)

(e)

(f)

There are several basketry stitches that can be used for securing coils. Here the figure eight, or Navajo stitch, was chosen, since it is an almost invisible method for joining coils.

As work continues, the weft will need to be replenished. To do this, a new length of yarn is laid on the core alongside the remaining weft, then both are covered with wrapping. Use this method when adding or changing colors. When several color changes are planned, new colors may be added without removing the existing weft. The first color is simply wrapped along with the core and may later be brought back to the surface as the design dictates.

Coiled jewelry may take many different shapes after the center circle is established. Three-dimensional shaping is achieved by changing the alignment of the coils. Round flat designs are produced by securing rows of coils side by side. Coils that are overlapped create a cylindrical shape.

A slight overlapping of coils is present in the disc-shaped pendant shown. A molded leather face, decorated with paint and feathers, was later applied to the textured coils of natural jute.

Adding weft in basketry:

(a) A new length of yarn is laid alongside the short weft.

(b) The new weft is wrapped over both ends. Photographs by Clark G. Adams.

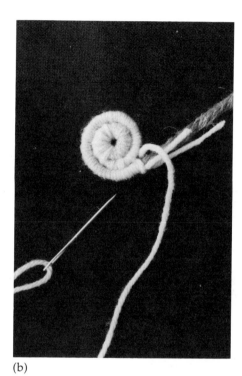

(b)

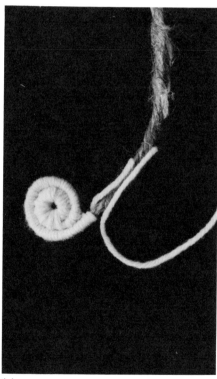

(a)

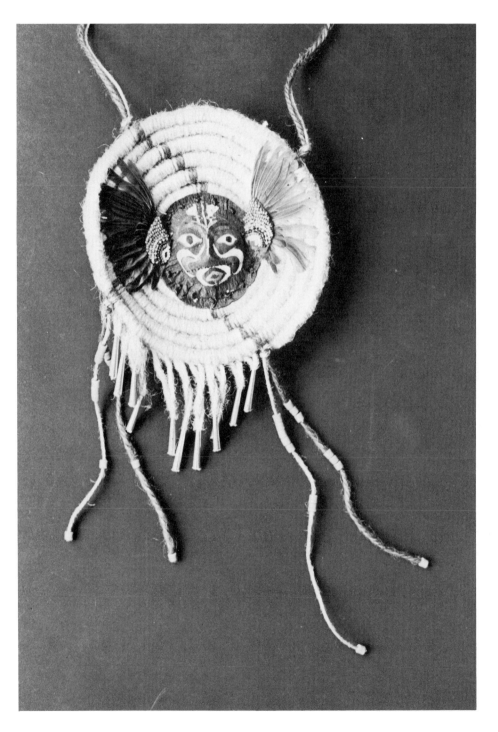

Molded leather face adorns disc-shaped pendant of natural jute coils. Artist, Ellen Jones.

The basic circular shape of the coil can be further modified by changing the direction of the core. As the core is doubled back on itself and secured with the figure eight stitch, a variety of elongated shapes result, allowing the designer to develop freeforms.

As jewelry from coiled basketry evolves, materials and techniques are adapted to meet individual inspiration. *In Flight* is an example of this adaptation. Begun as a circular basketry coil, the design expands with a dramatic sweep, from regular flexible core material to plastic welting cord. Exhibiting superb control of the media, the designer exposes the ends of plastic core contrasting them with the textured Lazy Squaw stitch used for the body of the necklace.

Shaping is made possible as the core is doubled back on itself and secured. Artist, B. J. Adams. Photograph by Clark G. Adams.

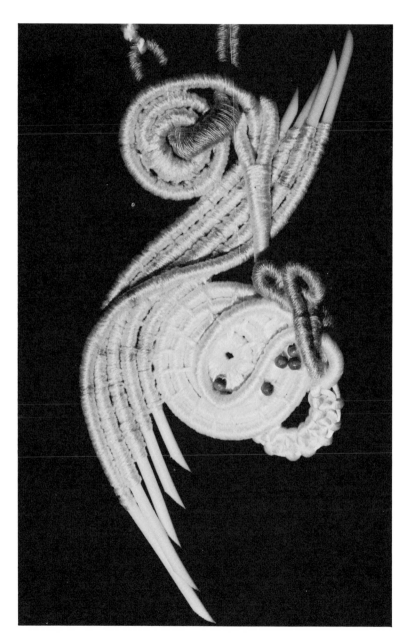

In Flight derives much of its dramatic impact from the interior core of plastic welting cord. Artist, B. J. Adams. Photograph by Clark G. Adams.

Knotted Tapestry

Contemporary macramé jewelry is most often visualized in terms of open patterns and complex knotting sequences. Knots are selected to produce texture and shaping. Designs are normally spontaneous and free flowing. For this reason it may be difficult to imagine macramé in the form of knotted tapestry, confined to alternating patterns of double half hitches. Nevertheless, knotted tapestry is an attractive medium for soft jewelry.

Designs for tapestry are first plotted on graph paper. As in all tapestry, the size of the yarn will control the amount of detail in the work. Designs knotted from very fine, closely tied yarns are comparable in detail to regular woven tapestry. However, contemporary geometric designs using medium weight macramé cord are most practical for an initial project.

The principle of knotted tapestry, or the Cavandoli stitch, is based on alternating Horizontal Double Half Hitches and Vertical Double Half Hitches. These two knots used in combination with two or more contrasting colors control the tapestry. As the Horizontal Double Half Hitch is tied over the knot bearing cord, the color of this cord is hidden, while the reverse is true when the Vertical Double Half Hitch is used.

Design ideas for jewelry may be developed by arranging cut shapes of colored paper into a cartoon. After the cartoon has been resolved,

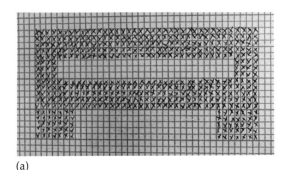

(a)

(b)

(c)

it is transferred to graph paper. Each square on the graph paper represents a single knot. Horizontal Double Half Hitches are designated with darkened squares; Vertical Double Half Hitches remain light. When completed, the graph will represent the pattern of the proposed tapestry.

Tapestry knotting is begun in the usual way. Double cords of the required length are attached to the holding cord with a Lark's Head. The number of cords to be used is represented on the graph. In this case, 16 double cords are required. As indicated by the graph, the first five rows of knotting consist of Horizontal Double Half Hitches covering the white knot bearing cord. The sixth row established the pattern with four Horizontal Double Half Hitches, followed by 30 Vertical Double Half Hitches, plus four more Horizontal Double Half Hitches to finish the row. The next two rows of knotting follow this same sequence. The remainder of the piece is comprised of Horizontal Double Half Hitches tied according to the graph pattern.

When knotting is completed, the holding cord is removed and the excess cord is turned under and basted to the back. The cords at the center, between the straps, are also trimmed, turned under and stitched. The knotted form is then lined with black felt.

Knotted Tapestry:

(a) Each square represents a single knot. Horizontal Double Half Hitches are designated with an X; Vertical Double Half Hitches remain unmarked.

(b) The Horizontal Double Half Hitch consists of two loops. The first hitch is looped under, around and over the white knot bearing cord and tightened. The second loop is then added in the same manner to complete the knot.

(c) In the Vertical Double Half Hitch, the white cord becomes the knotting cord and is tied over the vertical black cords. This knot also is formed from two loops. The first hitch is looped over the black cord, then around and through the first part of the knot. After the loop is pulled taut, a second loop is formed in the same manner.

(d) When knotting is completed, the white holding cord is removed.

(e) After excess is basted to the back, the knotted form is ready for lining.

(e)

(d)

Knotted tapestry choker is tied around the neck. Artist, the author.

Knotted tapestry may be finished numerous ways. The illustrated choker is one of the simplest. The loose cord ends that remain after knotting were trimmed to become ties for securing the tapestry choker around the neck. Knotted neck fastenings are also practical when they are planned to complement the tapestry design. A simple combination of Diagonal Double Half Hitches used with Horizontal and Vertical Double Half Hitches can provide shaping without visual clutter.

More eleborate fastenings, suitable for mounting three dimensional tapestry designs, might incorporate several unrelated materials. For example, plastic tubing, aluminum wire and metal grommets were employed to construct the neck fastening for the mixed media creation, *Birds of a Feather*. These same materials are integrated into the body of the neckpiece and serve as a receptacle for clusters of spiney feathers.

Birds of a Feather combining tapestry, feathers, plastic, soft aluminum wire, and grommets. Artist, the author.

Leather Molding

One of the great advantages of leather for jewelry making is its capacity to be shaped and formed by wet molding. The elastic quality of wet leather, plus its ability to retain a molded shape when dry, makes leather an irresistible medium for those who define jewelry in terms of a small sculpture.

Not all leathers are moldable. Take care to choose only vegetable tanned hides—medium grade cow hide of 4 to 8 ounces is usually recommended.

The process of wet molding is a simple one. The leather is soaked in water. The wet leather is affixed to a mold with rustproof nails and allowed to dry. The success of the process will depend upon the mold used for shaping and the designer's ability to transform shaped leather into a jewelry design.

Leather forming molds are constructed by carving a block of soft pine into the desired shape. However, other "found" molds can be just as effective. The illustrated example shows a piece of leather being molded around a wooden spindle taken from an old piece of furniture. This shape, like many others to be found, was discarded and free for the asking.

(a)

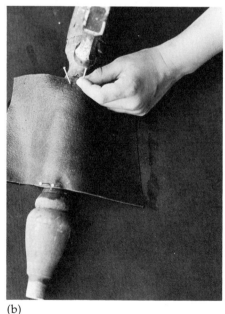

(b)

Leather Molding:

(a) Vegetable tanned leather is first soaked in water.

(b) Wet leather is tacked to a wooden mold using rustproof nails.

(c) Leather is allowed to dry on the mold.

(d) After drying, the leather retains its new shape.

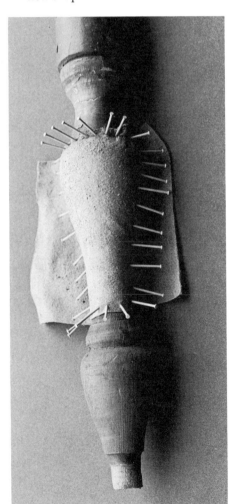

(c)

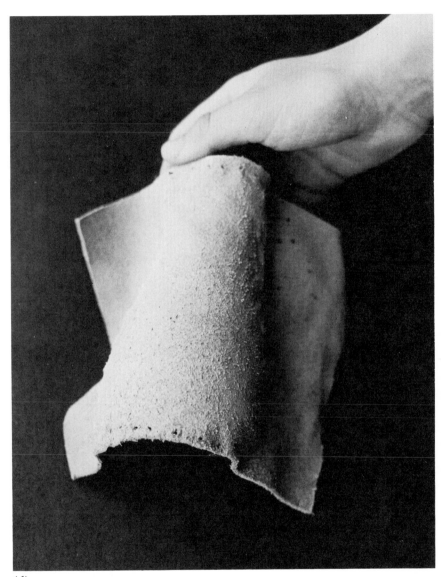

(d)

One or more molded leather pieces can be combined into a jewelry design. The necklace with the painted face exhibits two different types of leather molding. The heavy background leather was shaped over a found mold similar to the one shown earlier. Thinner leather was formed into the detailed face, with its bulging eyes and prominent nose, and required a special mold to produce the one-of-a-kind results.

Another molding technique that is now being practiced with great success is handformed leather molding. The wet leather is stretched and formed with the hands until it acquires the desired shape and then is allowed to dry.

The necklace illustrated is an example of a highly refined design statement produced by hand forming leather. The marvel of this technique is epitomized by the fact that the entire necklace was cut and formed from one continuous piece of leather.

Molded leather pendant with fur, feathers, beads, bone and seashells. Artist, Ellen Jones.

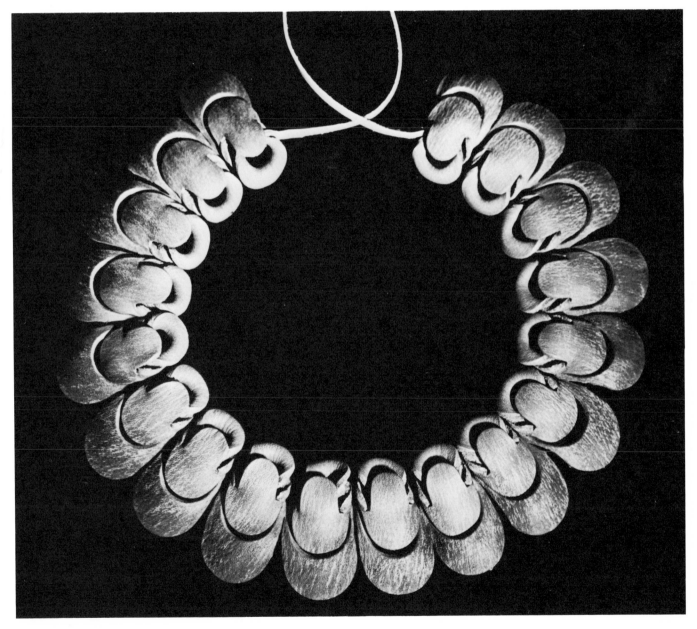

Hand formed leather necklace created
from one continuous piece of leather.
Artist, Daphne Lingwood.

Suppliers

Fabric

Local fabric shops, department stores and second-hand clothing stores

Bloomfield Woolen Co., Bloomfield, IN 47424   *Pre-cut wool strips*

Central Shippee, 24 W. 25th St.,
New York, NY 10014   *felt*

Homespun House, 9024 Linblade Ave.,
Culver City, CA 90230   *cotton*

Utrecht Linens, 33 Thirty-Fifth St.   *linen*
Brooklyn, NY 11232

Yarns and Fibers

Craft Yarns of Rhode Island, Main St., Harrisville, RI 02830

Lily Mills, Dept. HWH, Shelby, NC 28150

Mexiskeins, Inc., P. O. Box 1924, Missoula, MT 59801

Trait Tex Industry, Div. Colonial Woolen Mills, 6501 Barberton Ave., Cleveland, OH 44102

Yellow Springs Strings, Box 107, Yellow Springs, OH 45387

Leather

Scrap leather from local leather craftsmen

A.C. Products, 422 Hudson St., New York, NY 10001

Colo-Craft Leathercraft, 1310 S. Broadway, Denver, CO 80210

Sax Arts and Crafts, 207 N. Milwaukee, Milwaukee, WI 53202

Tandy Leather Co., 8117 Highway 80 W., Fort Worth, TX 76116

Additional Supplies

local plumbing supplies, hardware stores
and craft shops   *plastic, metal shapes brass and copper wire*

Bethlehem Imports, 1169 Cushman Ave.,
San Diego, CA 92110   *Beads*

Lambert Co., Inc., 920 Commonwealth Ave.,
Boston, MA 02215   *dye, printing inks*

Bibliography

Design

Aldred, Cyril. *Jewels of the Pharaohs.* New York: Praeger Publishers, 1971.

Coarelli, Filippo. *Greek and Roman Jewelry.* London: Hamlyn, 1970.

Cordrey, Donald and Dorothy. *Mexican Indian Costumes.* Austin: University of Texas Press, 1968.

Davis, Mary L. and Greta Pack. *Mexican Jewelry.* Austin: University of Texas Press, 1963.

Dayan, Ruth, with Uliburt Freinberg. *Crafts of Israel.* New York: Macmillan Publishing Co., 1974.

Dochstader, Frederick J. *Indian Art of the Americas.* New York: Museum of The American Indian, Heye Foundation, 1972.

Dongerkery, Kamala S. *Jewelry and Personal Adornment in India.* Delhi, India: Vikas International School Book Service, 1971.

Gerlach, Martin. *Primitive and Folk Jewelry.* New York: Dover Publications, Inc., 1971.

Fregnac, Claude. *Jewelry From the Renaissance to Art Nouveau.* New York: G. P. Putnam's Son's, 1965.

Morton, Philip. *Contemporary Jewelry.* New York: Holt, Rhinehart and Winston, Inc., 1970.

Mourey, Gabriel, et al. *Art Nouveau Jewelry and Fans.* New York: Dover, 1973.

Sieber, Roy. *African Textiles and Decorative Arts.* New York: Museum of Modern Art, 1972.

Willcox, Donald J. *Body Jewelry: International Perspective.* Chicago: Regnery, 1973.

Fiber and Fabrics

Belfer, Nancy. *Designing in Batik and Tie Dye.* Worcester, Ma: Davis Publications, 1972.

Belfer, Nancy. *Designing in Stitching and Appliqué.* Worcester, Ma: Davis Publications, 1972.

Cosentino, Geraldine. *Step-By-Step Bargello.* New York, Golden Press, 1974.

Gaines, Patricia Ellison. *The Fabric Decoration Book.* New York: Golden Press, 1973. William Morrow & Co., Inc., 1975.

Hall, Carolyn Vosburg. *Stitched and Stuffed Art.* Garden City: Doubleday, 1974.

Harvey, Virginia I. *Macramé: The Art of Creative Knotting*. New York: Van Nostrand Reinhold Company, 1967.

Harvey, Virginia I. *The Techniques of Basketry*. New York: Van Nostrand Reinhold Company, 1975.

Krevitsky, Nik and Lois Ericson. *Shaped Weaving*. New York: Van Nostrand Reinhold Company, 1973.

Lewis, Alfred Allan. *The Mountain Artisans' Quilting Book*. New York: Macmillan Publishing Co., 1973.

Laury, Jean Ray. *Quilts and Coverlets. A Contemporary Approach*. New York: Van Nostrand Reinhold Co., 1970.

Meilach, Dona Z. *A Modern Approach to Basketry*. New York: Crown, 1974.

Meilach, Dona Z. and Lee E. Snow. *Weaving Off-Loom and Related Techniques*. Chicago: Regnery, 1973.

Nieuwhoff, Constance. *Contemporary Lace Making*. New York: Van Nostrand Reinhold Co., 1975.

Rainey, Sarita R. *Wall Hangings. Designing With Fabric and Thread*. Worcester, Ma: Davis Publications, 1971.

Shears, Evangeline and Diana Feilding. *Appliqué*. New York: Watson Guptell Publishing, 1972.

Springall, Diana. *Canvas Embroidery*. London: Charles T. Banford Co., 1969.

Wildman, Emily. *Step-By-Step Crochet*. New York: Golden Press, 1972.

Wilson, Jean and Jan Burhen. *Weavings You Can Wear*. New York: Van Nostrand Reinhold Co., 1973.

Leather

Meilach, Dona Z. *Working With Leather*. Chicago: Henry Regnery Co., 1972.

Newman, Thelma R. *Leather as Art and Craft*. New York: Crown Publishers, 1973.

Willcox, Donald J. and James Scott Manning. *Leather*. Chicago: Regnery, 1972.

Mixed Media

Solberg, Ramona. *Inventive Jewelrymaking*. New York: Van Nostrand Reinhold, 1972.

Acknowledgments

I wish to express my thanks to all the students, art teachers and textile artists who contributed both time and ideas during the preparation of this book. Special thanks to Virginia I. Harvey, artist, author and Preparator of the Costume and Textile Collection, University of Washington, for the Foreword of this book, Joan Michaels-Paque, artist, author and teacher, Ruth Pearson Culbertson, Associate Professor of Art, Oregon College of Education, Monmouth, Oregon; Marjorie Schick, Assistant Professor of Art, Kansas State College, Pittsburg, Kansas, Katherine Crossman, Associate Professor of Art, University of Wisconsin, Whitewater, Wisconsin; (Mr.) Merle H. Sykora, St. Cloud State College, St. Cloud, Minnesota; Ramona Solberg, Associate Professor of Art, Univeristy of Washington, Seattle, Washington; Dorothy Zopf and Joyce Rupert, art teachers, Yellow Springs Public Schools, Yellow Springs, Ohio; Rex Lingwood, Halifax, Nova Scotia, Canada; B. J. Adams, Washington, D. C.; Lucretia Romey, Canton, New York; Bucky King, Sheridan, Wyoming; and members of Fibres 'n Friends fiber cooperative, Centerville, Ohio.